1536895

J
296.19   Patterson, Jose.
P   Angels, prophets, rabbis & kings from
        the stories of the Jewish people / text
        by José Patterson ; colour
        illustrations by Claire Bushe. -- 1st.
        American ed. -- New York : P. Bedrick
        Books, 1991.
           144 p. : ill. (some col.) ; 28 cm.
           Includes index.
           ISBN 0-87226-912-4

           1. Folklore, Jewish. 2. Bible
        stories--O.T. I. Bushe, Claire, ill.
        II. Title III. Title: Angels,
        prophets, rabbis, and kings from the
        stories of the Jewish people.

        23 JAN 92   22860642   APRGxc   90-23469

ANGELS, PROPHETS, RABBIS & KINGS

from the

STORIES

of the

JEWISH PEOPLE

ANGELS, PROPHETS, RABBIS & KINGS

from the

STORIES

of the

JEWISH PEOPLE

TEXT BY JOSÉ PATTERSON

Colour Illustrations by Claire Bushe

PETER BEDRICK BOOKS

NEW YORK

THE AUTHOR
José Patterson's extensive experience in special
education led her to a writing career. After many years
of primary school teaching, she took an Oxford
University Postgraduate Diploma in Special
Educational Studies and from that time worked in
Traveller Education. After being Teacher-in-Charge of
a mobile school for Gypsy children for three years, she
was appointed Regional Adviser for Traveller
Education in Oxfordshire and Berkshire. Articles on
aspects of her work have been published in leading
education journals and she has written four children's
books.

THE ARTIST
Claire Bushe comes from Scotland and after taking a
BA in Theatre at Dartington College of Arts worked as
a dancer and choreographer in film and theatre. She has
always painted and began working as an illustrator after
success in an illustrators' competition sponsored by a
major magazine. This is her first book.

Frontispiece
The illustration on page 2 is from 'Rabbi Israel
laughs' (p.106).
Line illustrations by Edward Ripley (pages
7,11,16,21,32,41,49,62,70,86,105,113,127,134) and
Claire Bushe.

Library of Congress Cataloging-in-Publication Data
Patterson, Jose.
    Angels, prophets, rabbis & kings from the stories of the
Jewish people/text by Jose Patterson: colour illustrations by
Claire Bushe.
    Includes index.
    Summary: A collection of traditional Jewish legends from
the earliest times, stories of the rabbis, and tales from the
communities of medieval Europe.
    ISBN 0-87226-912-4
    1. Legends, Jewish. 2. Bible. O.T.—Legends. 3. Aggada. 4.
Jewish folk literature. [1. Folklore, Jewish. 2. Bible stories—
O.T.] I. Bushe, Claire. ill. II. Title. III. Title: Angels,
prophets, rabbis, and kings from the stories of the Jewish
people.
BM530.P33 1991   90-23469
296.1'9—dc20   CIP
                                            AC

First American edition published 1991 by
Peter Bedrick Books
2112 Broadway
New York, NY 10023

Printed in Italy
5 4 3 2 1

Contents

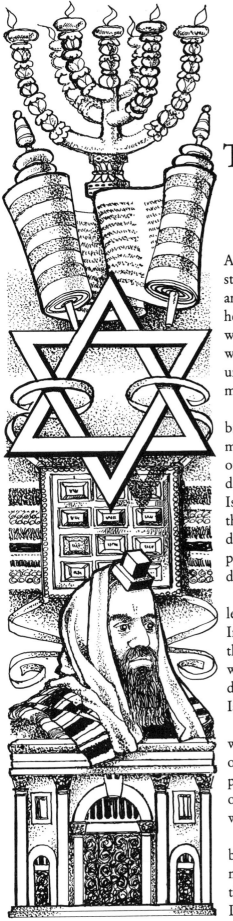

The Jewish heritage

Angels, Prophets, Rabbis and Kings, are not the only figures in the stories and legends of the Jewish people. There are also patriarchs and princesses, sages and saints, hassidim and tzaddikim, heroes and heroines, rogues and sinners, and many more, all of whom are woven into the great, rich tapestry of traditional and folk literature which has become an integral part of the Jewish heritage. The long unbroken golden thread running through this fine brocade is monotheism—the belief in one God.

The narratives of the Hebrew Bible, written in a tantalizingly brief style, cover the story of the creation and the early history of mankind. Spanning a period of nearly two thousand years they tell of God's Covenant with Abraham, Isaac and Jacob and their descendants, known as the Hebrews, the Children of Israel, or Israelites. In essence this is the story of how Israel won its land, then lost it and won it again. Side by side with the possession and dispossession of their land, the great leaders strove to keep the people together through the laws and code of behaviour written down in the Ten Commandments.

Some time about 2000 BCE the Patriarch Abraham and his family left the city of Ur of the Chaldees in Mesopotamia (now southern Iraq) and travelled westwards to the land of Canaan, later known as the land of Israel and, from Roman times onwards, as Palestine. It was there that Abraham's son Isaac, his grandson Jacob and the descendants of Jacob's twelve sons formed the twelve tribes of Israel, each with their own portion of land.

Later, famine drove them out of Canaan to Egypt where they were welcomed by Joseph, one of Jacob's sons, who had become an official of the Egyptian King or Pharaoh. The Pharaoh gave them permission to settle, and for a time they prospered, but in the course of time the Israelites suffered under cruel and despotic Pharaohs who oppressed them and made them slaves.

Under the outstanding leadership of Moses, inspired and guided by God, the Children of Israel escaped from Egypt and spent the next forty years wandering in the wilderness where God gave them the Ten Commandments. Eventually they returned to the Promised Land of Canaan. The twelve tribes became independent of one another and vulnerable to attacks from neighbouring peoples such as the Philistines. Through the efforts of the prophet Samuel, the tribes were united to form a kingdom, and around 1025 BCE Saul was elected as their first king. He was followed by David, who consolidated the kingdom and made Jerusalem its capital. He was as famous for his music and poetry as for his military victories.

David was succeeded by his son Solomon under whom the kingdom reached its greatest prosperity. Solomon built the first Temple—a magnificent edifice—in Jerusalem, which became not only the central place of worship, but a focal point for pilgrimages during the great religious festivals. Jewish traditional literature abounds with stories of David's exploits and Solomon's wisdom.

After Solomon's death the kingdom divided into two: the northern kingdom of Israel, sometimes known as Samaria, and the southern kingdom of Judah, with Jerusalem as its capital.

The northern kingdom went through a troubled period and was finally overthrown about 722 BCE by the Assyrians, who drove most of the inhabitants into exile. The Kingdom of Judah continued to be independent until it was invaded by the Babylonians under King Nebuchadnezzar. In 586 BCE Jerusalem was conquered and the Temple destroyed. The tragedy of the destruction of the Temple is commemorated in the Book of Lamentations in the Hebrew Bible.

It was during the time between the fall of the Kingdoms of Israel and Judah that great prophets like Isaiah, Amos and Micah made their powerful utterances and encouraged the people to put their faith in the one true God. These exhortations were timely because the Israelites had begun to worship other gods and the prophets foretold that God would destroy their kingdoms as a punishment.

The northern kingdom was never restored but in 538 BCE the Israelites were allowed to return to Judah and rebuild the Temple in Jerusalem, under the leadership of Ezra and Nehemiah. In 445 BCE the Temple once again became the religious centre of the Jewish people. It was at this time that a group of scholars called 'the men of the Great Assembly' explained the details of Jewish laws and customs to the people and laid the foundations of the religious practices which are followed to this day.

The country was conquered again in 332 BCE by Alexander the Great but the Jews were allowed to continue to practise their own religion. However, a hundred and fifty years later the country was overrun by Antiochus of Syria. He not only denied the Jews their religious freedom, but desecrated the Temple with idols and forced the Jews to worship foreign gods.

Sickened by Antiochus' religious persecution an aged priest, Mattathias, supported by his five sons, started a revolt of small, poorly-armed bands of Jews called Maccabees. They fought a guerilla war in the hills surrounding Jerusalem and under Mattathias' third son, Judah, eventually drove out the Syrian army, marched back into Jerusalem and rededicated the Temple. This victory is commemorated in the Festival of Hanukkah, which is still celebrated every year.

This newly won independence was not to last, for the Maccabees were unable to keep the people united. The Romans who were fighting in neighbouring Syria took advantage of the internal confusion and unrest and captured Jerusalem in 63 BCE. Palestine later became part of the Roman Empire.

The Roman rule was harsh and cruel and although the Jews retaliated with a series of rebellions they were no match for their enemy. In CE 70 the Romans destroyed both the Temple and Jerusalem, killing many of its inhabitants and driving the rest into exile. This tragic period in Jewish history is still commemorated by fasting and prayer on the ninth day of the Hebrew month of Ab. From that time until the new State of Israel was established in 1948, Jews were scattered all over the world with no homeland of their own.

The loss of the second Temple was a watershed in the history of the Jewish people. The dispersal of the Jews was called the Diaspora or the Exile, and from then on their life and literature reflected their great longing to return to their homeland. Wherever Jewish communities settled and developed they became more dependent on religious scholarship, and Academies of Jewish learning were established where the history and customs of their people were studied.

After the Roman conquest many Jewish scholars and leaders fled to Babylon in Mesopotamia, which became one of the great centres of learning, almost as influential as Jerusalem had been. One version of the Talmud, a central and most important work of sacred literature, second only to the Hebrew Bible, was compiled in Babylon, the other in Jerusalem. The Talmud, which is explained in more detail in the chapter 'Tales from the Talmud', contains laws, narratives, history, fables, prayers, ethics, moral sayings, as well as philosophical and religious discussions.

The frustrating lack of information in the Hebrew Bible is more than adequately compensated for by another great body of material written about that time in Hebrew and Aramaic known as the Midrash, which means 'commentary'. The Midrash sets out to interpret the texts of the Bible and comprises moral teachings, stories, legends and commentaries of all kinds which attempt to fill in what the Biblical narrative is so careful to leave out. It was compiled in the thousand years when followers of Judaism—the religious and cultural tradition of the Jews—had to defend their beliefs from the influences of foreign civilizations, from the invasion of Alexander the Great in the third century B C E to the Muslim conquests in the eighth century C E.

From Babylon Jewish scholars travelled to North Africa and Spain, and wherever they went they revived interest in Jewish studies and strengthened the Jewish faith.

Spain at that time was governed by the Moors—Moslem people of north-west Africa—and between the tenth and thirteenth centuries the Jewish communities prospered and flourished there. The Jews were allowed to hold high positions in the government, and there were many famous Jewish poets, philosophers, scientists and teachers who made an important contribution to the country. This period is known in Jewish history as 'The Golden Age in

Spain'. Perhaps the most renowned Jewish philosopher and theologian of this time was the great Maimonides. Once again their good fortune came to an end when, after the Christian reconquest, the Jews refused to convert to Christianity and were expelled from Spain in 1492.

Jews also settled in northern Europe and some came to England as traders at the time of William the Conqueror, but they were expelled by King Edward I. They did not return until the middle of the seventeenth century when a learned rabbi, Menasseh ben Israel, appealed to Oliver Cromwell that the Jews be allowed to return. Once again the Jewish people settled in England and were given freedom to practise their faith.

The fortunes of the Jewish people varied in Europe, where at different times they were allowed to live in peace and follow many different occupations. In the main, however, they were subjected to religious persecution and repression when they were not allowed to own property and forbidden to follow normal trades.

Life was particularly difficult for the Jews during the period of the Crusades (the eleventh to the thirteenth centuries), when many thousands were cruelly massacred by the Crusaders on their journeys through Europe to Palestine—the Holy Land, which the Crusaders were fighting to reclaim from the Muslims. The Crusaders, staunch supporters of Christianity, helped to spread hatred of the Jews, who from the sixteenth century were forced to live in ghettos and to wear a yellow badge to distinguish them from their Christian neighbours.

In the aftermath of violent attacks upon the Jewish communities in Europe, many works of sadness and despair were written, but their experiences also produced a spate of folk tales in which saintly Jews were thought to have been given supernatural powers as a protection against the Jew-haters. Stories such as 'The Golem of Prague' spring from these difficult times.

From the end of the eighteenth century a new movement of religious fervour known as

Hasidism arose in eastern Europe and gave rise to an abundance of tales and legends glorifying the wondrous powers of the new religious leaders known as Tzaddikim. In eastern Europe Jews suffered even greater hardships under the Russian Tsars and from 1880 onwards they were persecuted mercilessly. Thousands were massacred in pogroms—anti-Jewish riots—and as a result almost two million left Russia to settle in western Europe and America.

At about this time a movement named 'Lovers of Zion', was founded whose members wanted to return to Palestine and begin a new life there. The young idealists, known as Zionists, began to farm the neglected wastelands and lived together there in settlements. Jews all over the world were inspired by Theodore Herzl, the great leader of Zionism, and by many outstanding leaders who followed him, and tried to persuade various governments to set up a Jewish state in Palestine where the Jewish people would be free to live in peace.

In 1917 the British Government issued the Balfour Declaration which officially supported the Zionist Movement and recognized the right of the Jewish people to build their national home in Palestine. The Balfour Declaration added a new impetus to thousands of immigrants and volunteers who came to Palestine and helped to build new towns and villages. The Hebrew language was revived and the Jewish spirit began to breathe freely once again in its ancient homeland. But growing Arab opposition led to increasing and complex difficulties.

In spite of strenuous efforts from Jews all over the world the Jewish National Home had still not been achieved when World War II broke out in 1939.

Adolf Hitler had come to power in Germany with an official policy aimed against the Jewish people. As he led his conquering armies through Europe he set up concentration camps for the purpose of murdering Jewish people. Between 1939 and 1945 six million Jews were killed, over one-third of the world's Jewish population. Not only the people, but all their institutions of culture and learning in Europe were destroyed. This terrible catastrophe is known as the Holocaust.

The new, small State of Israel was finally created in 1948 and thousands of homeless Jews settled there to begin a new life. The Hebrew language, which for centuries had been used only in prayer, began to be used for everyday speech and is now the official language of the country.

For more than three thousand years, the Jewish people, in spite of persecution and every kind of setback, have maintained their ethnic and cultural identity, and their literature and folklore faithfully reflect these historical experiences.

The sacred writings of the Hebrew Bible, the Talmud and Midrash contain an inexhaustible supply of stories, legends, myths and parables of the Jewish people. By the humanizing art of the storyteller such great heroes as Moses, David and Solomon, and prophets like Elijah, Isaiah and Jeremiah have been transformed into well-loved kinsmen. And even God has lost his awesomeness.

By and large the rabbis were down-to-earth teachers of the people, endowed with good practical sense. In their desire to make their teaching intelligible to ordinary people they adapted familiar tales and legends which they cleverly wove into the fabric of their learned discourses and discussions.

Jewish folklore touches on Heaven and Earth, Paradise and Hell, Good and Evil, the natural and the supernatural, the spiritual and the material, the sacred and the profane. Many stories show the influence of other nations, such as Persia and Babylonia where the Jews lived for many centuries in exile.

Nevertheless, although the sources of the stories may vary, they have certain unifying and distinguishing features. They are full of brave humour, wit and irony and they are invariably pious. The writers of Jewish tales rarely missed an opportunity to point a moral lesson, to offer consolation and hope, and above all to inspire their readers with a pride in their people and an implicit trust in God.

Readers of all ages in every generation have enjoyed these stories—and it is to be hoped that they will continue to do so.

The creation

The first book of the Hebrew Bible is called Genesis, a word which means 'beginning', 'creation' or 'origin'. The Book of Genesis goes back to the beginning of time, telling how God created the world and the first man and woman.

In six days God made everything in the universe: first light and darkness, which He called Day and Night. Next came the Heavens, followed by the seas, and dry land, which He called the Earth. Then he made trees and plants of every kind, the sun, moon and stars, fishes and birds, mammals, insects and reptiles and lastly, in His own image, He made man. Man was formed from the dust of the Earth and God breathed the breath of life into his nostrils to make a living soul. Everything was finished in six days and on the seventh, when the great work was completed, God rested. He called this the Sabbath Day and sanctified it and made it holy.

God's great work, recounted so briefly in Genesis, gave rise to a treasury of folk literature, and the *Midrash*, one of the collections of Jewish writings where the stories are recorded, is full of imaginative accounts which fill in additional details of the events of creation and explain aspects of Jewish beliefs and customs. To make the explanations easier for people to understand, the writers sometimes gave personalities and characters to abstract concepts. The Torah, (the Law of the Jewish people) becomes a living, speaking being while the Earth, the Sun and the Moon—even the letters of the alphabet—all speak and behave in very human ways.

In the beginning, it is said, two thousand years before the Heaven and the Earth, seven things were created.

The Torah, written with black fire on white fire rested in the lap of God; the Divine Throne; Paradise on the right side of God, Hell on His left; the Celestial Sanctuary, with a jewel engraved with the Name of the Messiah on its altar, was placed in front of God, and there was a Voice that cried aloud, 'Repent, you children of men.'

When God decided to create the world, He first consulted with the Torah. She advised Him as follows: 'Almighty God, a king without courtiers and attendants and lacking an army hardly deserves the name of king, for he has no one to give him the honour he deserves.'

God was well pleased with this counsel, and from then on he taught all earthly kings, by His own example, not to undertake important decisions without first consulting their advisers.

The advice of the Torah was not given lightly for she had many reservations, not the least of which was the whole question of the value of the earthly world. Knowing the sinfulness of men, she felt they would be sure to disregard her commandments. However, God himself removed her doubts. Through the path of repentance, sinners would have the opportunity to mend their ways. Paradise and Hell would act as reward and punishment, and the Messiah was appointed to bring salvation, and put an end to evil.

The letters of the alphabet

To understand this story, you need to know that the Hebrew alphabet has twenty-two consonants and ten vowels, and is written from right to left. Each Hebrew letter stands for a number—Aleph is one, Beth is two and so on. The *Tephillin* that are mentioned are also called Phylacteries and are worn by religious Jews. They consist of two leather cases—one of which is strapped on the head and the other to the arm. In each are pieces of rolled parchment on which are written prayers, including the daily prayer, which is called the *Shema* and proclaims the Unity of God.

According to the Midrash, when God was about to fashion the world He sat on His magnificent throne to consider His plans for creation, and consulted the Torah, just as an architect consults his blueprints for building a house. Engraved with a flaming pen around the base of His crown were the twenty-two letters of the Hebrew alphabet. One by one the letters freed themselves from the holy crown and came down to stand before God. They jostled and argued and vied with each other for His attention, calling out 'Almighty God, create the world through me.'

The letter Tav pushed to the front and said, 'I have every good reason to be chosen to lead the world for my letter stands at the beginning of the word Torah. The time will come when Moses will give the Torah to the Children of Israel.'

And God replied, 'That is true, and in three thousand, three hundred and six years' time I shall command that you, letter Tav, will head the word *Tephillin* which will serve as My symbol and be worn on the forehead of the good and righteous. When the destroying angel comes to punish the sinners, he will see the Tephillin on the men of God and do them no harm.'

But the letter Tav was only partially consoled by God's words and left His presence.

One after another the letters of the alphabet pleaded their cause, explaining why they above all others should be attached to words of the utmost importance. God listened patiently to their petitions before turning them down.

Then the second letter of the alphabet, which is called Beth, spoke to God and said, 'O Lord God, the daily prayer in Your praise begins, *Baruch*—which means Blessed—Blessed be the Lord for ever. Surely there is no better justification for using me?'

And the Lord God was pleased with these words and took the letter Beth for *Baruch* and also placed her as the first letter of the Hebrew words *Bereshit Bara*—'In the Beginning He Created. . .'

During all this time God noticed that the letter Aleph had stood quietly in her place. 'Why are you the only one who has asked nothing of me?' He asked her.

And Aleph answered, 'Lord God of the Universe, I am the least among Your letters, and since my number value is only one, it is hardly fitting that I should make any demands.'

God was so impressed by Aleph's modesty that He told her: 'Because you esteem yourself so lightly you shall become the foremost among the letters. It is true that your value is one, but God is One, and the Torah is also One. And when My People receive the Ten Commandments, which are the essence of the Torah, I will use your letter to introduce them.'

And so the letter Aleph is pronounced first in the Hebrew word *Anochi*, which means 'I am the Lord Thy God.'

The envious moon

Long, long ago at the beginning of time there was a great emptiness, without shape or form. When God decided to create the world, everything changed. The first world was not to His liking, nor the next one, and God made and destroyed many worlds before the one we live in was made. Then God stretched out His right hand and made the Heavens. Then He put out His left hand and made the Earth. And this time He was well satisfied with the results.

But the Earth was dark and barren, covered only with bare mountains and deep seas. 'Almighty God,' the Earth sighed, 'I am quite alone down here. The Heavens are near to You whereas I am far away with nothing but great hard stones and the cold, fathomless seas for company.'

God's reply was swift: 'You are right. You will soon be surrounded by all kinds of living things—grass, fragrant flowers, trees and bushes. Your fruits will nourish man and beast, you will enjoy listening to the songs of the birds, and children's laughter will give you great pleasure. You will never be alone again.'

And the Earth was content and thankful.

When God made the Sun and the Moon, the darkness vanished in a moment and the world was bathed in a wonderful light. God created the Sun and Moon on equal terms—in size and power they were the same and although they took it in turns to light up the sky they each shone for the same length of time.

Nevertheless the Moon was dissatisfied. 'Lord of the Universe, you have created me and the Sun and endowed us both with a great light. But the people have no means of knowing which is the Sun and which the Moon. Besides I do not think that the Sun's radiance should equal mine,' the Moon grumbled.

'Would you like greater strength?' asked God.

'I think it would be better if the Sun's rays were weaker,' replied the Moon, 'and I hope you can help me in this matter, just as you helped the Earth with her problem.'

God grew thoughtful. 'I am faced with dissension and envy which I am forced to punish. If I allow it to go unchecked, it will gradually destroy My beautiful world.'

Then he looked at the Moon and answered firmly, 'I will settle the matter in My way. Because you envied the Sun's light, you will always be in its shadow. From now on your light will be dimmed and you will be easily recognizable—everyone will know that the lesser light is the Moon.'

Then He added, 'But you will share your brightness with hundreds of thousands of stars who will be your close companions.' God looked sternly at the Moon. 'What the Earth requested was fair and just,' He said, 'but your request is born of envy.'

No sooner had God finished speaking than the Moon began to grow smaller, its light dimmed and thousands of stars appeared.

The Moon was full of self-reproach. 'Dear God,' it sobbed, 'have pity on me and forgive my vanity.'

'It is too late! I cannot go back on my word.' And then God felt compassion for the repentant Moon. 'But I will give you distinction in the following way: From now on the Jewish people will number their days, months, weeks and years by you, the Moon.'

And ever since that time the Jewish people have arranged their lives by a lunar calendar. Unlike other nations, they do not begin to count the hours of the day from the sunrise, but from the appearance of the first three evening stars. And when the Moon is new, the Jewish people, prayer books in their hands, stand in its light and say a special prayer to God.

When the Moon hears the Creator being praised, then, and only then, does it forget its sin of long ago.

The arrogant sea

When God first made the seas, the waters began to rise so fast that they almost reached the Throne of Glory. And God called out: 'Stop! Waters—be still!'

But the waters were vain, pompous and dangerous. They boasted: 'We are the mightiest of all God's creation—let us flood the Earth!'

When he heard this God became angry and threatened, 'Unless you put an end to your arrogant boasting, I will send the sands to form a barrier against you.'

When the waters saw the size of the tiny grains of sand they began to mock and sneer: 'How can anything so small and fragile stand up to the likes of us? Why even the smallest ripple will wash them away.'

The grains of sand were uneasy, but their leader comforted them. 'You have no reason to fear the great waves. Listen to me. It is true that we are insignificant when looked at one by one, and that we are at the mercy of the wind, which can blow us to every corner of the Earth. But if we all remain together, the waters will see that we are a power to be reckoned with!'

The little grains rallied to these words of encouragement. And, as if a secret signal had been sounded, the sands of all the Earth came flying in from every direction. They lay down one on top of the other and against each other, layer upon layer, along the shores of the seas. They rose up in mounds, in hills, and in mountains, and formed a vast, solid barrier.

And when the waters saw how the immeasurable number of grains of sand had united against them they were subdued and retreated to their allotted place.

Adam and Eve

The Book of Genesis tells how God formed Adam from the dust of the Earth and breathed into his nostrils the breath of life, so that he became a living person.

Then God created a beautiful garden, a kind of paradise, called the Garden of Eden, which He filled with flowers and trees. In the middle of the garden God placed two trees—the Tree of Life and the Tree of the Knowledge of Good and Evil.

Adam's task was to cultivate and care for the Garden of Eden. God gave him clear instructions that he could eat the fruits of every tree in the Garden, except those from the Tree of Knowledge. These were strictly forbidden and the penalty was death.

Next, God provided Adam with a helpmate and partner. To achieve this God put Adam into a trance-like sleep. While he slept, God took one of his ribs and created Eve from it. Adam and Eve were both naked, but they felt neither shame nor embarrassment.

Life in the Garden of Eden was pleasant enough, until one day a cunning serpent suggested to Eve that she should pick the forbidden fruit from the Tree of Knowledge. When she protested that she would die if she did so, the serpent was quick to explain that not only would she not die, but she would learn the difference between good and evil, and become as wise as God Himself.

Eve listened to the snake and was sorely tempted. She picked the delicious fruit and ate it and then gave some to Adam.

As soon as they had eaten the fruit they looked at each other in a different way. They felt humiliated and self-conscious about their nakedness and quickly made rough garments from leaves in an attempt to cover themselves.

When the All-Seeing God saw Adam and Eve, He knew exactly what had happened and he punished them all for their disobedience. The snake was condemned to crawl in the dust and dirt forever, and Adam would always have to work hard with the sweat of his brow. Eve did not escape God's anger: for her there would be the pain of childbirth. And God banished them from the beautiful Garden of Eden for ever.

The Bible account of the creation of human beings is probably the best known of all stories. Over the centuries, countless legends have been woven around it. One tells how when the Almighty wished to make man He first consulted His ministering angels.

'I will create man in our image,' He told them.

The angels had never heard of man and they were full of curiosity: 'What is this creature called Man, what does he do and what is his purpose?' they asked.

'He will see that justice is done,' God replied.

Then a furious argument broke out among the angels, who were equally divided in their views. One group agreed with God that man should be created, while the second was opposed to the whole idea.

The Angel of Forgiveness spoke in favour: 'I think man should be created, for I know he will be generous and benevolent.'

But the Angel of Peace objected, 'If you make man, he will be constantly at war.'

The Angel of Justice was optimistic. 'Man will bring justice into the world.'

The Angel of Truth had nothing good to say. 'Do not create man, for he will be a liar.'

God became impatient with them all, especially Truth, whom He flung down from Heaven to Earth. Then, in spite of all the protests and objections, God created man. 'Tomorrow you will see for yourselves that man is your superior in wisdom and knowledge,' he told his angels.

Then the Creator gathered together all kinds of wild and tame animals, the many different species of birds and flowers of every shape and size. He asked the angels to give them names, but they were unable to do so.

So God said to them: 'Now you will witness an example of man's intelligence for he will succeed where you have failed.'

And sure enough when man saw the birds and animals and flowers he arranged them in categories and found a name for them all. 'And what shall I call you?' God asked him. 'My name,' said man, 'should be Adam because You have created me from *adama*—the Earth.'

The angels

In Jewish traditions and folklore angels are supernatural beings who live in Heaven, acting as God's messengers, carrying out His divine commands of reward and punishment. Like courtiers of a king, they form the divine council which surrounds the Celestial Throne.

The angels work in Heaven and on Earth and some travel constantly between the two. It is believed by some that for every thought and action of man there is a corresponding good angel or evil demon.

The angel Akatriel stays close to man in order to hear his deepest and most secret thoughts, which he then relays to God. Sandalfon, who is said to be so enormous that it would take five hundred years to reach the top of his head, weaves celestial crowns out of man's prayers.

Most of the ministering angels live only a short time, but others, including the seven archangels, enjoy a long life. These are Michael, Raphael, Gabriel and Uriel who have their own special positions around God's Heavenly Throne, and Metatron, Sandalfon and Nuriel who are hidden from view.

Michael, whose name in Hebrew means, 'who is like God', is the high priest of the angels, and stands on the right side of the Celestial Throne. Gabriel's name means 'strength of God' and he stands to its left. He deals with divine justice and punishes the wicked. Uriel, meaning 'splendour of God', is in front of the Throne, while Raphael, meaning 'healing of God' stands behind it.

Metatron is responsible for keeping order in the world. He is a dazzling figure, with veins of fire and flaming flesh. He was given seventy-two wings, thirty-six on each side of his body. He has thousands of eyes, each one as bright as the sun. God ordered him to protect the Throne of Glory, and before anyone can enter the seven-roomed palace where God resides, they must first pass Metatron, of whom everyone, even Samael, the Prince of Darkness, is afraid.

At first Samael recognized God as his superior, but later he was joined by other angels in a rebellion against the Almighty. A terrible war was fought between the armies of Samael and the forces of the great angel Michael, ending in Samael's defeat. The vanquished angels were condemned to the realms of the dark underworld.

But that was not the end of Samael's influence. He caused death to come to the human race. Samael is always the first one on the scene of death and destruction.

In order that men may receive the reward and punishment they deserve for their actions, God gave man free choice. Because of that He purposely allowed Samael the freedom to lead them into temptation. When Samael succeeds he appears before the Heavenly Court in the role of accuser and prosecutor. But, fortunately for man, Samael's powers are ultimately controlled by the merciful God.

The great flood

The story of a flood which overwhelmed the world is told in the legends of many peoples all over the world. The best known version is the story of Noah and the flood, which appears in the Book of Genesis in the Hebrew Bible.

Many generations had passed since Adam and Eve had been sent out into the world. Over the centuries, men and women turned away from God and each generation became more wicked than the last. Eventually, the people were so corrupt and wicked that God came to regret that they had ever been created. He decided, therefore, that He would destroy mankind and every living creature by means of a great flood.

Now at this time there was a righteous, God-fearing man called Noah who had a wife and three sons, Shem, Ham and Japheth. God recognized Noah's goodness and made plans to save him and his family. He commanded Noah to build a wooden ark according to His specific instructions. Noah and his sons worked long and hard, in spite of onlookers who scoffed when they saw the huge boat, three decks high, standing on dry land. When at last the ark was completed Noah took his wife and family inside.

Then God spoke to Noah: 'And you shall bring living creatures of every kind into the ark, two of each kind, a male and a female of every bird, beast and reptile. See to it that you take sufficient stores of food for you all.'

Noah obeyed all God's commands and listened very carefully to His warning: 'In seven days' time I will send rain for forty days and forty nights, and I will wipe every living thing that I have made off the face of the earth.'

Everything happened as God had decreed. For forty days and nights the rains poured down until the mountains disappeared beneath the flood and every living thing perished. Everything, that is, except Noah, his family and the animals, for as the waters rose, the ark was lifted up on the surface and floated away with its strange cargo safe inside.

For months the ark floated alone on the vast, empty waters. Then, gradually, the waters began to recede, mountain tops became visible once more and the ark grounded on Mount Ararat. Seven days later

Noah opened the window and released a raven; but it soon returned, having found nowhere to land. Another seven days passed and this time Noah set a dove free. Again, the bird returned to the ark. Next day he sent it out again and this time it returned in the evening carrying an olive leaf in its beak, a sure sign that the waters had subsided still further. A week later Noah released the dove for the third time and when it did not return Noah knew that it had found a dry place to perch.

The time had come for Noah to bring his family and all the animals out of the ark. As soon as he was once again on dry land, Noah built an altar and made sacrifices and gave thanks to God for his mercy. And God promised that He would never again flood the earth. And as a constant reminder of this promise to His people He set His bow—a rainbow—in the sky.

Noah and his sons cultivated the soil and planted vineyards, and his children peopled the earth again.

Falsehood and Wickedness

Many legends have been told about Noah, his ark and the creatures he saved from the flood. The following tale explains how falsehood and wickedness managed to survive even though the evil world where they had flourished had been destroyed. The story begins before the coming of the great flood.

As soon as Noah had finished building the ark, he gathered together two of every kind of animal and creature and watched carefully to see that they went into the ark in pairs.

And according to God's prophecy, the flood waters rose, the Angel of Death appeared and normal life came to an end. It was at this time that Falsehood realized that she would soon be out of work. Once the rising flood waters had swept away all the sinners, she would be left without any customers. But where could she go for safety? At the last moment she hurried to the ark, only to find the entrance firmly closed. She knocked with a trembling hand and Noah put his head out of a window in the side to see who was there. Being a righteous man, Noah did not recognize Falsehood. 'What do you want?' Noah asked.

'Please let me in,' pleaded Falsehood.

'Go and find one of your own kind, then I will let you both in,' Noah told her. 'As you can see there is room only for those with a mate or partner. These are God's rules which everyone here must obey.'

Falsehood turned away, bitterly disappointed, wondering whatever would happen to her now. She had not gone far when she met her old friend Wickedness, who, like her, was now without work.

'What have you been doing with yourself, Falsehood?' Wickedness asked.

For once Falsehood was compelled to speak the truth. 'Noah has just turned me away from the ark because I am alone. It seems that permission to enter is granted only to pairs of creatures. I don't comply with the rules so he won't let me in,' she explained.

Wickedness swallowed, coughed, and with a twinkle in his evil eye he asked, 'Now, my dear friend, are you really telling me the *truth*?'

'Of course I am,' Falsehood protested. 'I would be safely inside the ark by now if it were not for the rules.' Then she thought for a moment. 'Why don't you join me, Wickedness, so we can both be assured of a place. What do you think?'

Wickedness thought the matter over. 'What will you give me if I agree to your proposal?' he asked.

'I will give you everything I earn,' Falsehood offered. 'I do very well from the proceeds of my lies so you have no need to worry.'

Wickedness agreed immediately to these terms and without further delay a formal agreement was drawn up and duly signed and sealed. As soon as they had finished their business they went to see Noah, who allowed them both to enter the ark.

In no time at all, Falsehood had begun to spread her lies and was busy from morning till night among the creatures in the ark. When she had a moment for reflection she thought of her contract with some regret. There was no doubt it was a one-sided agreement, for she alone did all the work.

The matter preyed on her mind and she determined to broach it to Wickedness at the first opportunity.

'I hope you appreciate how hard I work at my trade *singlehandedly*,' said Falsehood, emphasizing in no uncertain terms the unfairness of the agreement. Wickedness would not be drawn into the argument. He simply reminded her of their original terms, took all the money she made from her lies and recorded the sum total of each day's takings in his accounts book.

By the time the flood had receded and Noah, his family and all the creatures were able to come out of the ark, Falsehood had acquired great wealth, and Wickedness was quick to lay claim to it all.

Falsehood entreated him: 'Dear friend, please give me a rightful share of what I have earned. After all, I have done all the work.'

Wickedness gave her a contemptuous look. 'Did we not make a solemn agreement that I was to have everything you earned?' he demanded. 'How can you possibly think of asking me to break our contract now? You must admit it would be a very wicked thing to do, wouldn't it?'

Falsehood had no answer and went away, knowing full well that she had been foiled in her attempt to cheat her friend Wickedness. For there is much truth in the proverb: 'What Falsehood gains, Wickedness takes away.'

Noah and the animals

There is a legend which tells that the moment Adam, the first man on Earth, died, Noah was born with God's blessing and from that time life was much improved for the human race.

God had placed a curse on Adam and Eve which affected their whole lives—time and time again their wheat crops failed because they became choked with thistles and thorns. But the curse was lifted during Noah's lifetime and the land was fertile once more.

It was said that Noah also invented new ways of making life easier for men by teaching them to make their own ploughs, sickles, axes and many other useful tools.

When God ordered Noah to build the Ark he told him exactly how to construct it. It was to measure 300 cubits from stem to stern, 50 from side to side and 30 from the hatches to the keel. There were to be three decks, each of which was divided into hundreds of separate cabins to house all the different animals. The lowest deck was designed for the mammals, from the heaviest elephants to the smallest mice. The middle deck was kept for the birds and was made as light and airy as possible so that they would not feel too confined away from their natural element. The upper deck was for all the creeping things, the reptiles and the insects, the snakes and worms and caterpillars. There was also space on this deck for Noah and his family, for his wife, his three sons, Shem, Ham and Japheth and his sons' wives.

When Noah had at last finished building the Ark he turned his attention to assembling the animals as God had ordered. God decided to help Noah for he knew that his task was a very difficult one. For each species of animal God sent an angel carrying a basketful of its natural food in order to attract it into the Ark. Since Noah was unable to see the angel, it seemed to him as if the animals were moving into the Ark of their own accord.

God ordered Noah to sit beside the door in the side of the Ark and watch carefully as each creature entered. All those who bowed down as they passed him were allowed in, but those who remained standing or tried to get in without so much as a greeting were refused entrance. This also applied to violent animals, for God decided that only those who were able to exist peaceably together were to be saved.

In addition, space was found in the Ark for some very strange creatures. There were two monsters, far too large to fit into any of the cabins. One was the Reem, which swam behind the Ark, resting its nose on the deck. The other was the giant Og, who kept his head above the flood water by holding on to a rope ladder which hung down from the side of the Ark.

And so the Ark was filled and the chosen animals, birds and human beings were saved from the waters of the great flood.

The Patriarchs

The Patriarchs is the term used to describe the founding fathers of the Children of Israel—Abraham, Isaac and Jacob. Their stories are written in Genesis, the first book of the Hebrew Bible and scholars believe the events are set between nineteen hundred and sixteen hundred years before the Common Era.

Archaeologists have discovered records from Mari, on the upper Euphrates river, which date from the time when Abraham may have lived and which give information about the way of life of the desert tribesmen. There are also records from ancient Egypt (from the days of the Pharaohs of the fourteenth century BCE) which tell about the land of Canaan and show traders and warriors from different parts of the area.

The people of that time lived in walled towns and villages and outside the settled areas large numbers of people led a nomadic or a semi-nomadic existence. Travel was common, not only to find fresh grazing for their large herds of sheep and goats, but also along well-trodden trade routes which connected the ancient cities of Mesopotamia with the southern kingdoms of Egypt and Arabia.

Daily life was governed by a variety of long standing customs which laid down rules of behaviour at every stage. The father, as head of the family, had wide powers. Normally the eldest son succeeded him as heir to his position and his property. The father's blessing, passed on from father to son, was an important part of a son's inheritance and once given could not be revoked.

The Patriarchs were aware of the need for a deep personal faith in God who guided them through life and who encouraged them with His promises. It was they who introduced the idea of monotheism—the belief in a single God, instead of the host of pagan deities that were generally worshipped in the area. They also represent the first stage of the biblical narrative of how Israel won its land, then lost it and won it again.

Perhaps the reason why the stories of the Patriarchs remain fresh after thousands of years is because the founding fathers are so human! They are revered by the Jewish people not only because of their courage and heroism and religious faith, but because they, too, are subject to human frailty.

Abraham and the idols

Long ago at the place where the two great rivers, the Euphrates and the Tigris, merge, a people called the Chaldees lived in the country of Chaldea.

In those days idol worship was commonplace. People thought that these images, often elaborately carved in wood, clay and stone, were gods who would listen to their prayers and help them. Sacrifices were made to them and they were bought and sold like any other commodity.

A man called Terah, who lived in the town of Ur of the Chaldees, was not only an idol worshipper but traded in them as well. His shop contained carved images of many different gods and people came there both to buy and to worship the idols.

When he was away on business, Terah left his shop in the charge of his young son, Abraham. Despite his youth, Abraham was capable of deep and searching thoughts about the world. The more he looked around him the more he realized that the wonders of creation were the work not of shoddy idols, but of Almighty God.

One day he was thinking about such matters in the shop when his reflections were interrupted by a customer.
'How old are you?' asked Abraham.
'Fifty years old,' came the reply.
'With respect, sir,' said Abraham, 'it suprises me that a man of your age can bow down before a carved piece of wood that was made only yesterday! If you think seriously about this, you will not be tempted to buy one of these idols.'

The man looked long and hard at the young man. He realized that, for the first time in his life, he was hearing the truth. Without a word he left the shop—empty-handed.

Shortly afterwards a woman came in carrying a bowl of flour as a sacrificial offering, and placed it in front of one of the idols. As soon as she had left, Abraham took a stick and went round breaking up every idol in the shop; only the biggest one was left intact. Then, carefully, he propped up the stick in the hand of the remaining idol.

When Terah returned and saw the debris of wood, clay and rubble which littered the shop, he took hold of Abraham and shook him. 'What on earth has been going on here? Who did this? I turned my back for a short time and what do I find on my return? Total destruction! Have you gone mad?'
'Be calm, Father, and I will tell you what happened,' said Abraham. 'A woman came into the shop with a bowl of flour as an offering. She put it down in front of one of the idols. As soon as she left, the place was in uproar. The idols started shouting and arguing, each one claiming that the flour was meant for him. None of them would listen to reason, and before long a violent fight broke out. And right in the thick of it, in an attempt to create order, the biggest idol picked up a stick and. . .Well, you can see for yourself what happened—he smashed them all!'
'You stupid fool,' Terah bellowed at his son. 'How can you possibly look me in the face and say such a thing. That idol smashed the others? You know as well as I do that they cannot move or speak or understand?'
'My dear father, you have spoken the absolute truth. This great universe was created by Almighty God—not by hollow idols.'

And so Abraham came to believe that there is only one, universal God and he and his family no longer worshipped the many gods of the Chaldees or traded in the idols they honoured.

The sacrifice of Isaac

Abraham married his wife, Sarah, in Ur but after some years he took his family and his father north, to Harran. From there God commanded him to travel south, to the land of Canaan. They lived as nomads, travelling with their flocks of sheep and goats, settling for a time wherever grazing was plentiful, then moving on again to a new area. After many years of marriage, Sarah, to their great delight, gave birth to a son, Isaac.

Isaac was Abraham's cherished heir, the son

for whom they had waited so long, and the years during which Abraham and Sarah watched him grow were filled with pleasure and joy. The child was regarded as nothing less than God's miracle and Abraham never forgot his gratitude to Him for His great blessing. Then, without warning, everything changed.

As long as he lived Abraham could never forget the night when God spoke to him: 'Take your only son, Isaac, whom you love so dearly, to the land of Moriah to a mountain which I will show you, and offer him as a sacrifice.'

Abraham was dumbfounded. He put his hands over his ears in an attempt to shut out God's command. But nothing helped. Every other thought was driven out of his mind and in its place, like the blows of a hammer, he could hear, over and over again, those five terrible words: 'Offer him as a sacrifice'. He was convinced that God was testing his faith. 'But surely He has no cause to doubt me, His faithful servant?' Abraham despaired.

Like a man in a ghastly dream he made the necessary preparations for his long journey, carefully concealing the truth from Sarah. 'God has commanded me to go to Mount Moriah to offer up a sacrifice,' he told her. 'It is a good distance from here and it may keep me from home for a few days. I will need to take two of our servants and Isaac too—for company,' he added in as matter-of-fact a voice as he could manage.

Sarah had no reason to be suspicious. 'Isaac will enjoy the journey. But I will miss him,' she sighed wistfully.

Early the following morning the men chopped the wood for the sacrificial fire and loaded it, together with some provisions, onto two asses. As soon as the other animals were saddled, Abraham and Isaac rode off, followed by the servants and the pack animals.

Isaac was very excited about the long journey ahead and chattered away endlessly to Abraham and the men. He was too busy asking questions to notice how changed his father was. Abraham answered the boy abruptly—quite differently from his usual patient way of explaining things. Then he rode ahead of the others, silent and deep in thought.

They travelled at a steady pace throughout the day, only stopping long enough to eat and to feed and water the animals. At night they pitched their tents under the stars and Abraham prayed to God, hoping for some sign; but none came.

On the third day they reached the foot of a high mountain which Abraham recognized as Mount Moriah. Abraham dismounted and spoke to the men: 'Wait here with the animals until we have prepared the sacrifice and worshipped God. Isaac, you come with me.' He helped the boy shoulder the bundle of firewood, while he carried his knife, a rope, and the clay pot containing the glowing coals. Slowly they made their way up the mountain path. Abraham knew that every step brought him nearer and nearer to the dreadful moment when he would have to make the supreme sacrifice.

'Oh dear God,' he said to himself, 'how ready I would be if You were to ask me to be Your sacrifice and spare my son Isaac.' But God was silent.

They walked on until they saw, in the middle of a level clearing, a large slab of stone worn flat with age.

'Pile the wood up over there,' Abraham told Isaac. 'We can use the top of the stone as an altar.'

The boy worked fast and when the wood was carefully arranged he jumped down from the stone and looked around.

'Everything is ready now except the lamb for the sacrifice,' he said, looking at his father. 'How strange that you should forget that.'

Abraham strained every nerve and sinew in his body to control his feelings. He put his hands on the boy's head and looked into his eyes.

'God will provide the lamb,' he whispered gently. 'You must do as I say without question, just as I obey God.'

The boy's lips went tight and he stood still while his father, trembling with emotion, took the coil of rope and tied Isaac's hands and feet. 'Why does God want me for the sacrificial lamb?' Isaac looked at his father again and saw that tears were running down his face. Abraham covered the boy's eyes and gently tied his arms with cord. Then he picked him up in his arms and placed him carefully on the pile of wood. Steadying the child's body with his left hand, he took the knife in his right and held up his arm, poised and ready.

At that very moment God called out to him: 'Abraham, Abraham!'

'I am here, Lord,' he answered. And then he thought his heart would burst when God spoke the most wonderful words he had ever heard: 'Do not raise your hand against the boy, do not touch him. I know now that you are a true God-fearing man since you were willing to give Me everything—even your only son.'

Abraham snatched his son from the altar, and hugged and kissed him and tore him free from his bonds. Then a scuffling noise in the bushes disturbed them. They looked round and saw a ram kicking and struggling, caught fast by its horns in the branches of a thicket.

'Look! I told you that God would provide the sacrifice,' Abraham shouted with joy. They managed to tie up the animal and offered it on the stone altar as a sacrifice, and both father and son worshipped God with heartfelt prayers. Then Abraham called the name of the place *Adonai Yireh*, meaning 'God Will Provide.'

And God spoke to Abraham a second time: 'Because you have obeyed My command and were ready to offer your only son to Me, I will give My blessing to you and your descendants for ever, and they will become as numerous as the stars in the sky and the grains of sand on the sea-shore.'

And Abraham pulled Isaac close to him and put his arm round his shoulder, and together they walked down the mountain.

The story of Jacob and Esau

Like Abraham before him, Isaac waited a long time to become a father and he was no longer a young man when his wife Rebecca gave birth to twin sons, Jacob and Esau. Isaac now owned his own flocks of goats and sheep, and moved around from place to place in search of good pasture land. But by the time Jacob and Esau were growing up, the family had pitched their tents and settled in Beersheba.

The two young men were very different both in looks and character. Esau, the elder of the two by only a minute, was a redhead, outgoing, rough in his ways and a keen hunter. He liked nothing better than to take his bow and arrows and go off on a hunting expedition for days at a time. His brother was quite the opposite. He was earnest, thoughtful and quiet, and preferred to lead a more settled life with the family and help his father with the livestock. Jacob had a close attachment to his mother, while Esau was his father's favourite.

In those days, before a man died he would bequeath the largest share of his possessions to his eldest son, as well as giving him authority to become the future head of the family. This was known as 'birthright'. To her dismay, Rebecca realized that all these rights and privileges would go to Esau, because he was the first-born twin, whereas Jacob, whom she considered to be more suitable to succeed his father, would have nothing.

Jacob did not like the situation at all. The truth of the matter was that he was jealous. Not only would his brother's inheritance be a substantial one, but in addition he would receive the special blessing which God had given to Abraham and his descendants. And while Jacob cared deeply about family responsibilities, Esau did not. He was first and foremost a hunter.

When, on one occasion, Esau had been away hunting for longer than usual, he returned home exhausted and faint with hunger. He saw Jacob cooking some food for his evening meal—a kind of thick lentil stew which was simmering gently over the fire. The air was filled with a most appetizing aroma from the herbs and spices—mouth-watering to a famished man.

'Jacob!' Esau moaned as he squatted down on the ground in front of the fire. 'I'm starving! That stew has a most wonderful smell and I would give anything for a large bowl of it!'

'Anything?' asked Jacob as an idea flashed into his mind, and a sinister glint appeared in his eyes.

'Yes, anything; but don't bother me with

questions now,' Esau answered weakly.
'You may have all the stew you can eat,' said Jacob, 'if you give me your birthright.'
'Oh, take it, take it, it will be of no use to me. Unless I get some food, I shall die of hunger.'

Jacob ignored his brother's remarks. 'Swear an oath that you will give me your birthright,' he insisted.

So Esau swore an oath. It was only later, when he had eaten his fill and the gnawing hunger pains had gone, that he realized just what he had done: he had sold his birthright for a bowl of lentil stew. Then he stood up, stretched, went to his tent and fell deeply asleep and thought no more of the matter.

The years passed and Isaac grew old and frail and blind. One day he called Esau to his bedside.
'My dear son, I am weak and tired and my end is near. But before I die I want to give you God's blessing, not just for you but for your children and their descendants.' Then he raised himself up on his pillows. 'I haven't much of an appetite these days, but I have a longing for venison. Take your bow and arrows and bring me some deer, and I will bless you on your return.'

Esau hesitated as if he was going to speak, then thought better of it. He bent down and kissed his father and went off, without telling the old man anything about the sale of his birthright to his brother.

Unknown to either Isaac or Esau, Rebecca was busy in an adjoining tent and overheard the conversation between father and son. Without a moment's hesitation she left her work and hurried off to find Jacob.
'I have thought of a plan,' Rebecca announced after she had explained to him what she had heard. 'Your father must feel that he has not much longer to live, otherwise he would not dwell so much on giving God's blessing. But I know a way for you to get it. We must act quickly. Listen carefully and do as I say. Go to the flocks and bring me two young goats and I will make Isaac's favourite dish, just as he likes it. When you have served it to him and he has finished eating, then you can ask for his blessing.'

Jacob was quick to see that Rebecca's scheme was not as simple as it seemed. 'Esau is a hairy man while my skin is smooth, and Father is bound to feel the difference when he touches me.' He lowered his voice. 'And when he finds out he has been tricked he will curse, not bless, me.'

Rebecca sprang to his defence. 'I will take the blame, my son. Let the curses fall on my head. Now hurry! Go and bring me the goats. I will prepare everything you need.'

There was much to be done and no time left to consider the consequences of their conspiracy. Jacob killed two young goats and Rebecca used them to prepare her husband's meal. While it was cooking, she found some of Esau's clothes and gave them to Jacob to wear. Then she cleaned the animal skins and draped them carefully over Jacob's arms and on the smooth nape of his neck. When everything was ready they entered Isaac's tent. Jacob carried the savoury dish and freshly baked bread and Rebecca brought the wine. Jacob laid the food beside Isaac's bed and knelt down.

Not everything worked quite according to plan. Isaac was pleasantly surprised to find that his meal had been prepared so quickly. But something troubled him. He thought he heard Jacob's voice, for the old man's sharp hearing compensated for his lack of sight.
'Is that you, Esau?' Isaac asked.
'Yes, father,' Jacob answered, trying hard to imitate his brother.

Isaac stretched out his hands and when he felt Esau's hairy arms and smelled the distinct odour of the fields on the hunter's robes he was finally convinced that this was indeed his favourite son.

When he had finished eating and drinking Isaac placed his hands on Jacob's head and blessed him.
'May God send you dew from heaven,
And the richness of the earth,
New wine and an abundance of grain.
A curse upon those who curse you;
And a blessing on those who bless you!'

And when Jacob and Rebecca had said Amen, they left Isaac content and drowsy from the food and wine.

They had scarcely left Isaac's tent when Esau returned. He called out: 'Father, I am home! Wait till you taste the venison. It will be cooked to perfection! And the wine is excellent! Come, I will help you to sit up and then you can eat, drink and enjoy it all, and afterwards you can give me your blessing.'

Isaac roused himself. 'Who is there? Who are you?' he called out and his groping hands trembled with agitation.

'I am Esau, your elder son. Father, what is the matter?'

'Esau, Esau,' Isaac repeated slowly, 'then who. . .' The old man recovered himself sufficiently to tell Esau everything that had happened.

When his father had finished speaking Esau bellowed at the top of his voice—a sound full of fury, bitterness and rage. He cradled the broken-hearted old man in his arms and sobbed, 'This is the second time my brother has robbed me. He stole my birthright and now he has cheated me out of my blessing.' Then he implored Isaac, 'Bless me too, Father.'

'Alas, my son, I have only one blessing to give and Jacob has taken it by treachery. He has the rights, the honour and the authority and you must serve him.' Then he steadied himself and continued: 'But there will surely come a time when you will break away and be free of his domination.'

As soon as Isaac was sleeping once more, Esau crept away quietly. He went straight to Rebecca and faced her. 'I have a message for Jacob. Tell him that as long as Father lives he is safe. When he dies and the days of mourning are over, I will kill him.' And he turned and left the tent without another word.

Rebecca was afraid. Isaac could die at any moment and she feared for Jacob's life for she knew that Esau's words were spoken from the heart. She ran to Jacob.

'My dear son, for your own safety you must leave home at once. Go to Harran and stay there with my brother, Laban. I will send word when your brother's anger has died down and he feels ready to forgive you.'

Jacob, too, was frightened by Esau's threat to his life, and after hurried preparations had been made, he was about to leave when his mother called him to Isaac's tent and Isaac, too, advised him to go. Then the old man's heart softened and he gave Jacob a new blessing of his own, passing on to him the blessing God had given to Abraham, the hope of the Promised Land.

As Jacob walked away across the sparse desert he reflected on the recent events. When the sun had set and he could walk no further he found shelter from the cold night air in a rocky hollow. He took a smooth stone to use as a pillow, wrapped his cloak around him and lay down to sleep.

Until the day he died Jacob was never sure whether he had a dream or a vision that night. Whatever it was, it made a vivid and lasting impression. Resting on the ground by his head and stretching upwards to the glowing heavens, Jacob saw a ladder—a stairway thronged with people in shining robes. Some were going up and others coming down in a kind of gliding motion. Jacob knew at once that they were angels. Then God stood beside him and spoke. 'Jacob, you are not alone,' He said. 'I am the Lord, the God of your grandfather Abraham and your father Isaac. I will give lands to you and your descendants and they will multiply and spread throughout the world. I will bless and protect you and wherever you may wander, I will bring you back to this land.'

Then the bright lights faded into the darkness and Jacob woke up just as the dawn was breaking. He was stiff and cold, alone and afraid but he felt comforted when he remembered God's words. He used his stone pillow for an altar, and called the place Beth-El which means House of God. And Jacob prayed to God and made a vow:

'Dear God, protect me on my journey and help me safely back to my father's house, and I will make this altar into a holy place and I will give a sacred tithe—a tenth part of everything I have—for an offering.'

With that he continued his journey until at last he came to Harran, the home of Laban, his uncle. Jacob did not know then that many years would pass before he would be able to return home and there would be peace between him and his brother.

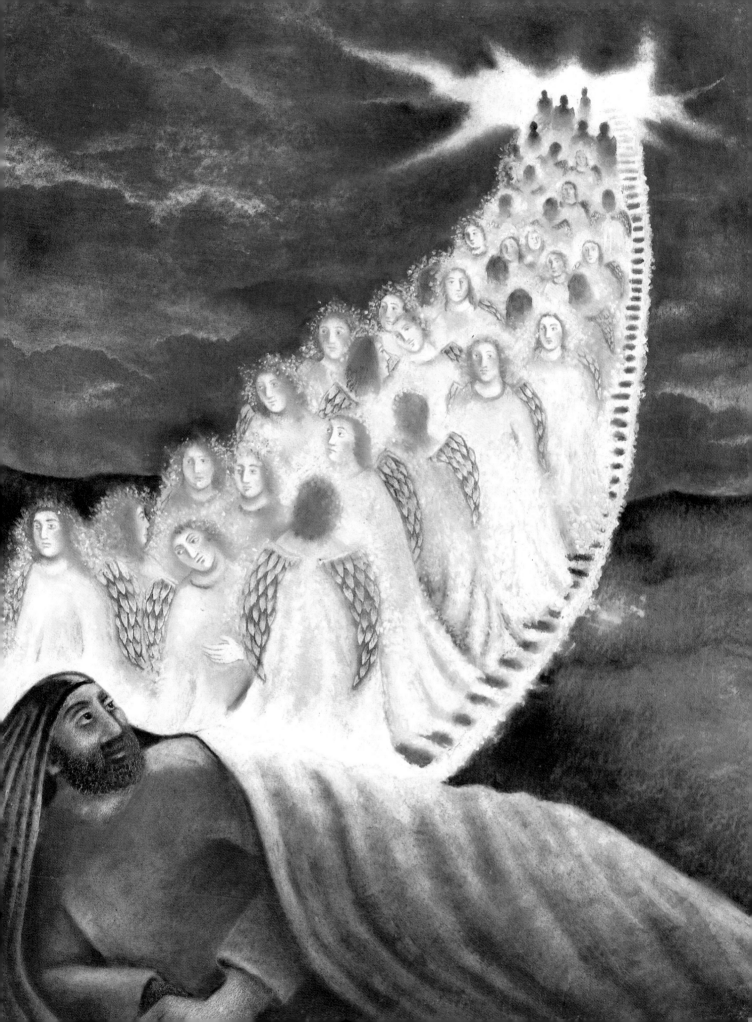

Joseph's story

Jacob settled at last in the Hebron Valley, some distance north of Beersheba and became a rich man, the owner of many sheep, goats and asses. He had a large household to support but they were willing enough to help their father look after the livestock.

Jacob had no less than thirteen children, twelve sons and a daughter. All but the last two were born to his first wife Leah and, as was the custom of those times, to his two concubines. After an interval of several years, Joseph and Benjamin were born to Jacob's beloved second wife Rachel, who died after Benjamin's birth. These two boys, the sons of his old age, had a special place in their father's affections, and Jacob made no secret of the fact that Joseph was his chosen favourite.

At seventeen Joseph was thoughtful, clever and quick to learn. His father thought that nothing was too good for him and one day presented him with a beautiful new coat, woven from many different-coloured wools. Its long sleeves—so different from the tunic-type garments usually worn at that time—made it all the more special.

Such out and out favouritism was the root cause of bitter resentment among Joseph's older brothers. They rarely, if ever, had a good word to say about him and muttered behind his back. But there was another reason for their resentment. For some time Joseph had become interested in the interpretation of dreams. Much to his brothers' unconcealed irritation he would enter into long explanations about them, trying to decide whether they might foretell a good or bad event.

One night at supper time, unaware of his brothers' bad feelings towards him, Joseph eagerly began a full description of his most recent dream.

'I must tell you about a dream I had last night,' he said with enthusiasm and before anyone had time to interrupt he continued: 'It was harvest time and we were all working in a field binding sheaves of corn. And suddenly my sheaf stood straight up on end, and your sheaves gathered round in a large circle and bowed down low before it.'

There was an unpleasant silence, then Judah, one of the brothers, sneered, 'And are we to understand from this that one day in the future you will be a king and lord it over us—your elders and betters?' The feeling of hatred underlying his remark was thinly disguised.

One evening the following week, when everyone had finished eating, Joseph told them about another dream, not knowing that he was treading on dangerous ground. 'I had such a strange dream last night. Although everything was black as pitch the heavens were suddenly lit up by the sun, the moon and eleven stars—and they all bowed down to me!'

As far as Jacob was concerned, Joseph could do no wrong, but even he was rather disturbed by this. 'My son,' he cautioned, 'what does your dream mean? Are you suggesting that your entire family will have to serve you in some way?' And the old man shook his head in mild reproof.

As for Joseph's brothers, they were furious with the way their father indulged the boy instead of putting a stop to his embarrassing nonsense. And from then on they made no attempt to hide their jealousy.

Soon after this, Joseph's brothers drove the goats and sheep away from their camp, in search of fresh pasture. Joseph remained at home but one day, when the brothers had been away for some weeks, Jacob sent for Joseph. 'I have heard that your brothers are minding the sheep at Dothan near Shechem,' he said. 'I am anxious for news of them and the flocks. Go and see if everything is well and bring me back a full account as soon as you can.'

Joseph packed all the provisions he would need for the journey, then kissed his father and his young brother Benjamim and set off.

While the brothers were all busy with the sheep, one of them happened to look up, shaded his eyes with his hand and recognized Joseph in the distance. He called to the others: 'Here comes the Dreamer in his fancy coat! Perhaps he has come all this way to tell us another of his weird and wonderful dreams!'

Had Joseph appeared without being seen

from afar, things might have been different. But his brothers were given the advantage of enough time to think how much he was favoured and spoiled, and about the way in which he implied, through his dreams, his future superiority over them. They had all the reasons they needed for hating him. And then, almost to a man, they decided to kill him.

'That will certainly put an end to his dreams,' one of his brothers snapped, 'but we must act now while we have the perfect opportunity.'

There was, however, one dissenter. Reuben, the eldest, was the only one to speak up in Joseph's defence. 'Surely we can find another way,' he said in an effort to reason calmly with his brothers. 'It would be wrong to kill our own flesh and blood. We can throw him into the pit instead—after all the result will be the same—and we will be well and truly rid of him.'

They all agreed and Reuben, who felt some remorse, secretly planned to rescue his brother later when the others had moved on with their flocks. Meanwhile, Joseph, oblivious of the sinister plot, waved to his brothers and was about to give them the traditional greeting when he was overpowered, stripped of his coat and thrown into a deep dry well. He was bruised and sore and too stunned to move.

Congratulating each other on their swift action, the brothers sat down to eat and drink and consider their next step. All, that is, except Reuben who was called away to inspect an injured animal. During a pause in the discussion they heard the distant clang of camel bells and looking in the direction of the noise, they saw in the distance a string of heavily loaded camels coming towards them. Judah jumped to his feet. 'Reuben is right,' he declared. 'We have nothing to gain by killing Joseph and concealing his death. I have a much better idea.' He pointed excitedly to the approaching string of camels. 'That caravan will be loaded with oil, herbs, spices and all kinds of goods on the way to the markets in Egypt. No doubt we can interest the traders in a different commodity! I am sure they will deal in anything if the price is right—even slaves!' And Judah folded his arms and stood back to watch his brothers' reactions.

But there was no time to consider, or argue or reason. The caravan came to a halt and the brothers were soon engrossed in haggling with the Midianite merchants. Then, to everyone's satisfaction, a bargain was struck—Joseph was sold for the price of twenty pieces of silver! With the aid of a rope he was hauled out of the pit and, still numb with shock, forced to stumble along behind the caravan as it continued on its way south to Egypt.

The celebrations were cut short when Reuben returned. He had first been to the pit and was alarmed to find it empty. And when Judah explained and offered him a tenth share of the money they had received, he stared at it thoughtfully.

'Who is going to tell Father, and what are we going to say to him?' Reuben said slowly. The brothers did not answer. The full realization of what had happened began slowly to penetrate their minds.

But something had to be done. They killed a goat, tore Joseph's coat, soaked it in the animal's blood and took it back to Hebron. And there was no need to say anything. Jacob recognized Joseph's coat and at once assumed that, while on his way to his brothers, he had been attacked and killed by a wild animal.

Jacob wept bitterly over the death of his beloved young son. He refused to be comforted, for Joseph had been the light of his life and nothing could compensate him for his loss. 'I will go to my grave mourning for my dear son,' he said.

Now far away, Joseph was confused and appalled by his brothers' actions, but more than that he grieved for his father and wondered if he would ever see him again. The long journey only increased his pain, for despite his youth and strength he was exhausted from insufficient rest and the meagre rations of food.

When the traders arrived in Egypt they took Joseph to a slave market and sold him to Potiphar, a captain of the Pharaoh's guard. Joseph soon recovered and quickly adapted to his new way of life as a slave in the household of a high-ranking officer. Potiphar found in Joseph everything, and more, that he could expect of a servant. He was trustworthy, intelligent and responsible. And it was not long before Potiphar asked Joseph to take charge of his entire household.

Joseph worked hard in his new position, and all would have been well had it not been for Potiphar's wife. She became infatuated with her husband's young, attractive foreign slave, and made no attempt to hide her feelings for him. Joseph, who was loyal to his master, was most embarrassed by his wife's unwanted advances and carefully avoided her. Nothing could have infuriated her more! To be spurned by a mere upstart like Joseph wounded her pride and she was determined to take revenge.

She told her husband that Joseph had entered her room in order to force his attentions on her. And she showed him Joseph's robe, which she had stolen to use as evidence. Potiphar believed the trumped-up charges and ordered Joseph to be sent to prison.

Joseph now had every reason to despair. He looked back on his brothers' treachery and the way in which his master's wife had plotted against him. And although his prospects seemed at their worst, he prayed to God to keep faith with him.

Joseph, however, was not one to dwell on his own sorrows for long. He spent time with his fellow prisoners and listened to their grievances. His previous senior rank as master of the captain's household gave him a privileged position and he became an assistant to the chief jailer.

Now it happened that, due to some minor offence, the Pharaoh's chief butler and baker were thrown in jail and one night both had dreams that worried and unsettled them. When they heard that Joseph was able to interpret dreams they begged him to help.

In his dream the butler had seen a grapevine with its three branches full of buds. 'And the buds opened and then formed into clusters of ripe grapes,' the butler explained. 'I picked the grapes and squeezed them into the Pharaoh's cup. And when I looked, the juice had turned into wine which the Pharaoh drank.'

Joseph explained: 'In three days' time you will receive a pardon from the Pharaoh who will reinstate you as royal butler. Once again you will be in charge of his wine store and wait on him at his table.' Joseph added, 'When you are released, speak to the Pharaoh on my behalf so that I, too, may one day be free.' And the delighted butler gave Joseph his word.

Then it was the baker's turn. 'I was carrying three baskets on my head, one on top of the other,' he said. 'The topmost basket was full of tempting foods for the Pharaoh. Suddenly a flock of birds swooped down and ate everything up.' The baker looked intently at Joseph. 'Will I, too, have my job back in three days' time?' he asked.
'If my interpretation is correct, there will be no pardon,' replied Joseph solemnly. 'In three days time the Pharaoh will issue a decree to have you hanged.'

Joseph was soon to know that God was with him, for everything he had prophesied took place. The baker was hanged and the butler, pardoned, returned to the palace. But two long years were to pass before the butler had occasion to recall his promise to Joseph.

It happened that the Pharaoh was anxious about the meaning of two vivid dreams he had had. Like all superstitious people he thought they might forewarn him of some future disaster. But although he consulted many counsellors and respected advisers, no one was able to help. It was then that the chief butler remembered Joseph and told the Pharaoh of the man in the prison who interpreted dreams. Joseph was quickly sent for. He was given clean clothes to wear and brought to the royal palace. He bowed low to the Pharaoh and listened carefully to his account.
'I was standing on the banks of the river Nile watching seven fat cows grazing,' the Pharaoh said. 'Then seven lean and gaunt-looking cows appeared and, to my astonishment, they devoured the fat ones without changing their shape! In my second dream, I saw seven full, ripe ears of barley growing on one large stalk. Next to them were seven more, thin and shrivelled, and these ears swallowed up the fat ones, although in appearance they remained the same. My wise men are as perplexed as I am. Can you explain these dreams?' he asked Joseph.

'It is not I who can explain, but the Almighty,' replied Joseph. 'I am of the Hebrew faith and believe in one God. I will be guided by Him when I interpret the dreams for you.' Then Joseph began his interpretation: 'Egypt will be blessed with the richest crops ever produced, which will give seven years of prosperity and plenty. These will be followed by seven years of the most severe famine in the country's history. I advise you to plan now to create reserves for the lean years. There should be a campaign of careful planting of high-yield crops. Great storehouses and granaries should be built to store the grain, and overseers appointed to handle supplies and distribution when the lean time comes. In this way your people will survive the seven years of famine.'

The Pharaoh sat back on his throne and looked at the young man in amazement. He and his courtiers were all deeply impressed by Jospeh's interpretation.
'Since you have been moved by the spirit of your God,' said the Pharaoh, 'there is no other man as wise or as intelligent as you to carry out

this work.' And he hung his gold chain round Joseph's neck and took his own ring with the royal seal and put it on Joseph's finger. 'I hereby appoint you to carry out this work for me. From now on you will be second in rank to me, and the people of Egypt will obey your every word.'

And Joseph, who had been both a slave and a prisoner, rose to the most honoured position in the country. He became indispensable to the Pharaoh and embarked on the enormous task which he himself had advised. And God remained with Joseph and the work was carried out to perfection. And everything that Joseph had predicted came about. The bumper crops were safely stored away to be used in the years of famine, and the people of Egypt were saved from starvation.

And many years were to pass before Joseph's own cherished dream came to be realized. He was to be reunited with his entire family—they even bowed down to him before he revealed his identity—and he became reconciled with his brothers when they came to buy grain in Egypt.

Moses, the great leader

Moses, known as 'Moshe, rabbenu' (Moses, our teacher), was the greatest leader and lawgiver in Jewish history. God made him His messenger to bring the Children of Israel, who were slaves under Pharaoh, out of Egypt to freedom. During the long period when they wandered in the wilderness, Moses gave them God's Ten Commandments and helped the people to become a nation. He brought the Israelites within reach of the Promised Land—and although God gave him a glimpse of the 'Land of Milk and Honey', he did not live long enough to enter it. The story of Moses is written in the Book of Exodus, the second book in the Hebrew Bible.

The story of Moses begins many generations after the time when Joseph was taken as a slave to Egypt, in about the thirteenth century before the Common Era. When the famine Joseph had foretold spread northwards, Jacob and his eleven sons journeyed to Egypt to buy grain. There they were reunited with their brother Joseph and the crimes of the past were forgiven. The Pharaoh, who had promoted Joseph to the highest rank in the country, welcomed his family and invited them to stay. From that time on Jacob's descendants settled in Goshen to the north-east of the country, and, generation after generation, their numbers grew.

As the years passed the situation changed. The Israelites became increasingly numerous and the Egyptians were afraid of their influence. The Pharaoh who was ruling the country at that time was nothing less than a despot. His main preoccupation was inventing new and harsher ways of persecuting the Hebrew people in order to crush their spirit. They became slaves and were used as forced labour to build two great Egyptian cities, Pithom and Rameses. Immune to their suffering and hardship, the Pharaoh next issued the most terrible edict of all: he ordered the midwives who delivered Israelite baby boys to kill them at birth. The baby girls were spared.

During the time when these laws were being enforced there lived a man called Amram, his wife Jochebed and their daughter, Miriam. They also had a three months old baby boy. But their pleasure and joy was overshadowed by the fear that at any time the child might be discovered and killed.

Jochebed confided in her husband: 'Our little son is growing so fast that it is becoming more and more difficult to conceal him. I am afraid that someone will hear him. I have thought of a new hiding place—the River Nile! Tomorrow I will gather some rushes and use them to weave a basket—a floating cradle! Don't worry,' Jochebed reassured her husband, 'the basket will have several coats of tar to make it completely watertight. I will hide it among the reeds and Miriam can keep a watchful eye on it while she is washing the clothes in the river.'

The next day Jochebed cut down as many tall bulrushes as she needed and worked all through the night. And the baby looked comfortable and contented in his new cradle. Then early in the morning, Jochebed and Miriam walked towards the river, each carrying a basket. Miriam balanced the larger one filled with washing on her head, while her mother held the smaller one, covered with a lid, in her arms. Inside it was her little son. She found a secluded place to leave it, offered up a special prayer for the child's safety and returned home. Far enough away not to arouse suspicion, and yet within earshot, Miriam began her washing.

When all the clothes had been washed, Miriam straightened her back and wiped her forehead. Then she stiffened in alarm. The Pharaoh's daughter and her handmaidens were walking near the river bank, calling to each other and about to enter the water close to the place where her little brother lay hidden. And sure enough the royal princess spotted the basket tucked away among the reeds and sent one of her servants to bring it to her. When she opened the lid and looked inside and saw the baby crying, her heart was full of pity for the helpless child.

'Come and look!' the princess called to the others excitedly. 'Come and see this poor hungry baby. He was floating among the rushes in this basket. He must be a Hebrew child, but he is so lovely, I think I shall keep him.'

Miriam was near enough to overhear the conversation. She did not waste a moment. She ran over to the group of women who were admiring the baby and knelt down to the Pharaoh's daughter.

'Your Highness, I know a Hebrew woman who could suckle the baby. With your permission I will go and fetch her. She lives quite near here—it will only take a moment,' she added anxiously.

The princess agreed and Miriam picked up her basket of washing and ran home as fast as she could.

'Mother, mother, stop whatever you are doing, put on a clean robe and come with me. Quickly! I will tell you why later,' she gasped.

Jochebed was too surprised to argue, and in the time it took to reach the royal party, Miriam had explained everything. Jochebed presented herself to the princess who hired her as a wet-nurse, as it was called, to feed the child—her own son!

But it was not a passing whim on the princess's part. She genuinely loved the boy and decided to adopt him, thus saving his life. She called him Moses from a Hebrew word meaning 'to pull out', because the child had been taken from the River Nile. And Jochebed cared for Moses, and when he was old enough took him to live in the Pharaoh's palace to be educated together with the Egyptian princes.

Moses was wise and thoughtful and although no mention was made of it, he was fully aware that he was different from the others in the royal household. He knew that he was one of the Children of Israel, and that Jochebed, Amram, Miriam and the young Aaron were his closest relations. However, unlike the other Hebrew people, Moses was free to come and go at will. The result of that freedom was to change his life, for wherever he went he saw the appalling conditions under which his kinsmen had to live, and he was sickened by the cruel way in which they were treated.

One day Moses saw an Egyptian slave-driver beating one of the Hebrew slaves unmercifully. Suddenly filled with uncontrollable rage, he struck the guard and killed him. He looked round to make sure there was no one in sight, then he buried the body in the sand. When he had dusted his clothes as best he could, he returned to the palace, thinking, with grim satisfaction, that, for once, justice had been done.

News, especially bad news, travels fast, and it was not long before the Pharaoh himself came to hear of the circumstances surrounding the death of one of his guards. His daughter was quick to warn Moses.

'The Pharaoh is very angry. I cannot protect you in this matter and I know the king will make no exception.' Then she added meaningfully, 'As you well know, he does not share my love for you. If you wish to escape death yourself you must leave Egypt at once.'

Moses knew she was right. Her warning only served to confirm his own fears and as soon as he had made the necessary arrangements he slipped quietly away.

Out of slavery

Moses travelled for many weeks, following the caravan routes through the desert until he reached the country of Midian, to the east of the Red Sea.

One day as he was resting, a group of young women came to a nearby well to draw water for their animals. As they approached, they were threatened by some wild-looking shepherds who barred their way.

Moses was furious, leaped to his feet and shouted angrily at the men, 'Who do you think you are, treating these young women like that? They are perfectly entitled to draw water for their flocks. In fact I will do it for them myself—stand back!' And he pushed the astonished shepherds aside, and started to turn the handle of the well rope. It took several buckets to fill the water troughs for the thirsty animals and Moses continued to wind the bucket up and down until all were satisfied.

The grateful young women thanked Moses warmly and drove the sheep back to their village.

And what a clatter and commotion there was when they reached home and tried to tell their father about the kind Egyptian who had helped them! The young women—all sisters—were the daughters of Jethro, the village priest. As soon as the patient man could get a word in he asked, 'Do you mean to tell me that a complete

stranger defended you, hauled water for my flock, and yet you left him behind? Go back at once and invite him to eat with us. The least we can do is to show him hospitality.'

And Moses was pleased to accept their invitation and join the family for their evening meal. From then on he became a regular guest and in time married Zipporah, one of Jethro's daughters. And when their first son was born, Moses called him 'Gershom' which means 'a stranger there' for Moses said, 'I am a stranger living in a foreign land.'

Moses led a simple life caring for his young family and shepherding his father-in-law's flocks. The very nature of his work—driving the animals from pasture to pasture—meant that he was often far from home and always alone. One day he came to the foot of Mount Horeb. As the sheep climbed up the slope, nibbling and cropping the thorny bushes as they went, Moses followed behind.

Suddenly he stood still in amazement. In front of him was an incredible sight, unbelievable and yet certainly real. A single bush was on fire, the flames dancing merrily and the smoke rising upwards. The strange thing was that the branches were unaffected, and the leaves remained green—neither scorched nor charred! And then Moses remembered that the place was known as 'The Mountain of God', and as he took a step toward the bush, he heard a clear voice which seemed to come from the centre of the roaring flames. 'Moses, come no further. Remove your sandals for you are standing on holy ground.' As he stood there barefooted, Moses knew that he was in the presence of God. 'I am the God of Abraham, the God of Isaac and the God of Jacob,' said the voice and Moses covered his face, too frightened to look up.

'I have witnessed the terrible oppression of My people in Egypt,' the voice continued, 'and I have heard their outcry against their brutal slave-drivers. The time has come to end their torment and bring them out of Egypt to the land of Canaan, a land flowing with milk and honey. Moses, go and speak to the Pharaoh and bring the Children of Israel out of bondage.'

Moses dropped his hands from his face and,

although he stood motionless, his thoughts were racing from the impact of God's message. And he was full of doubts.

'Almighty God, who am I to go to the Pharaoh and bring the Children of Israel out of Egypt? Surely, it is an impossible task for one human being to undertake? Who will listen to me? Who will believe me? The Pharaoh hates his Hebrew slaves but surely he will not want to free them? And what proof can I give to the Israelites that I am Your messenger?'

And God spoke again to Moses. 'Throw your shepherd's staff on the ground.' As soon as Moses did so, the staff turned into a long snake. Moses' reaction was swift—he jumped back and kept his distance, for he had no love of snakes. 'Moses, do not be afraid, take the snake by its tail.' And when Moses lifted the snake it turned back into a staff.

Then God told him to put his hand inside his coat; when he pulled it out it was white and scaly—just as if he had leprosy. He repeated the movement and his hand was perfectly healed.

Moses was reassured by these signs but he still lacked self confidence. 'Dear God, I am not worthy to undertake this task,' he said, hesitating. 'It will be difficult for me to rally the people, for I am no orator—in fact I stammer when I get excited.'

'Do not be afraid, Moses. I am your God and I will help you. Your brother Aaron will be your spokesman. Now take your staff and return to your kinsmen in Egypt.'

And Moses drove the flock back to Midian and told Jethro of his wish to return to Goshen to see his family. Jethro provided asses and provisions for the long journey, and wished them well. And Moses, Zipporah and their children returned to Egypt to fulfil God's commands.

Half way across the desert they found Aaron, who had journeyed to meet them. Moses confided in him everything that had happened at Mount Horeb. Aaron told him that during his absence, a new Pharaoh had come to the throne of Egypt and was, if anything, even more of a tyrant than his predecessor.

Just as Moses had predicted, the Pharaoh refused Moses' plea to free the Children of Israel nor would he acknowledge that the request came from God. Indeed, in a defiant mood, he made life even harder for the poor slaves. He ordered the overseers to withhold the supply of straw used in making bricks. 'Let them collect their own straw, but make sure that they produce the same number of bricks each day,' he commanded.

The new burden was too much. The Israelites turned on the two men. 'We cannot tolerate any more suffering!' they shouted. 'You are to blame, you made the Pharaoh angry and God will judge you and punish you for this.'

Moses and Aaron visited the Pharaoh again. 'Who is this God of yours that I should obey him? Has He sent you a sign?' the Pharaoh scoffed.

This time Aaron threw down his staff, which immediately turned into a snake. But to his dismay a group of Egyptian magicians went through the same motions and the results were exactly the same! However, Aaron's snake ate the magicians' snakes and when it was lifted up, it turned back into his staff. All this failed to impress the Pharaoh, who remained unmoved.

Then, using Aaron as his spokesman, Moses told the Pharaoh, 'If you do not let my people go God will send ten plagues—each one will be worse than the last.' With that the brothers left the palace.

Moses had never doubted that the path to freedom would be a difficult one. He knew that the Pharaoh was testing both him and the power of God and he was not surprised when the warning was ignored. So Aaron lifted his staff again and all the water—in the River Nile, in the canals and in the wells—turned to blood. The news spread quickly that those living in the province of Goshen, the Hebrew people, were unaffected. But nothing would change the Pharaoh's mind.

When the polluted rivers and wells were returned to normal a plague of frogs was sent instead. They swarmed all over the country in their millions—but not in Goshen. Then the Pharaoh relented. He summoned Moses and told him, 'Pray to your God to rid us of these frogs and I will free the slaves.' But at the last moment he broke his promise.

Now God sent other plagues—first lice, then flies—which infested the animals and the crops until the country was threatened with ruin. Each time the Pharaoh agreed to free the slaves—and then went back on his word. And as Moses had warned, every new plague was worse than the last. The cattle died, the people were infected with terrible sores and boils, and violent storms flooded the crops. Then the sky became black with a swarm of locusts which swooped down on the fields and devoured anything that was left. After the locusts had done their worst, God sent a terrible black fog.

Moses appealed again to the Pharaoh who, in spite of the suffering the plagues had caused his own people, remained obdurate.
'God has sent me to warn you that in ten days time the firstborn child in every Egyptian family will die. The slaves will leave Egypt on the following morning whether you wish it or not.'

Then Moses called together the elders of the community. 'Listen carefully. The Angel of Death will visit Egypt in the night. Each Hebrew family is to kill a lamb and use some of its blood to daub the lintel and doorposts of their house. When the Angel of Death passes over Egypt he will not visit those houses which are smeared. And we will celebrate this day and call it "Passover", and we will tell every generation how we left Egypt, and how we escaped from slavery to freedom.'

Everything happened as Moses had predicted. The Angel of Death came to Egypt in the night and each firstborn Egyptian child was slain. Only the Hebrew households were spared.

The next day the Pharaoh summoned Moses and Aaron. 'Enough! Enough! I have had enough of plagues and misfortunes. Take your people, your cattle and sheep and leave here at once. And pray to your God to bless me!'

The Israelites needed no urging. They left in such a hurry there was no time to add yeast to the bread dough or wait for it to rise. The bread for the journey was baked as it was, unleavened, a flat hard biscuit called Matza.

Like a great army, family by family and tribe by tribe, the children of Israel left Egypt. And God guided them on their journey with a pillar of cloud during the day and a pillar of fire at night.

The Almighty had delivered the Israelites from slavery and they were enjoying to the full their first taste of freedom! They were almost mad with joy and happiness. But the celebrations died down as quickly as they had begun. The new life in the desert was hard. The daily route was tiring, often through bare, unfriendly country; the problem of daily food and water supplies for themselves and their livestock had to be overcome, and a safe place had to be found to pitch camp at night. And as if that was not enough, they were suddenly faced with a new and terrifying threat.

In spite of the last dreadful plague, the Pharaoh bitterly regretted his decision to free his slaves. He had depended totally on their labour for building his cities and now the construction sites were still and silent.

He summoned his army chiefs. 'They cannot have gone very far. They are many, and are slowed down by their animals. We will soon overtake them, and bring them back to Egypt. Prepare all your military divisions—soldiers, chariots and horses, at once.'

By the time the Pharaoh's chariots caught up with them, the Children of Israel had reached the shores of the Red Sea. They looked back in terror to see a vast army bearing down on them.

They were trapped! Not knowing what to do, they vented their fear and anger on Moses: 'We have no chance! We shall all be killed! We would rather be slaves in Egypt than die here in the wilderness.'

But Moses calmed their fears and reminded them to keep faith with the Almighty. Then God told Moses to wave his staff, and the sea parted, leaving a long dry path. On either side were sheer walls of water, held firm by the power of God.

A tumultuous shout rose from the Israelites as they began to cross the sea-bed and the pillar of cloud moved from the front of the column to the rear, thus obscuring them from the pursuing army. God blessed the Children of Israel with a safe passage. Not so the Egyptians. As they galloped along after the Israelites, the sea walls closed over them and they were drowned.

And thus the period of Israel's slavery in Egypt came to an end, and a new era of freedom began.

In the Wilderness

With their trust in God strengthened by the miracle at the Red Sea, the Israelites travelled on through the desert, never tiring of recounting the events of their wonderful escape. Nevertheless, within a very short time there were renewed complaints about food and water shortages. At one of their stopping places they found the water to be undrinkable. Moses prayed to God who told him to throw a certain log into the water—and immediately it became sweet and pure.

Still the harsh reality of hunger led the people to compare their present conditions with those they had left behind. 'We may have been slaves, but we always had plenty of bread to eat,' they muttered.

Once more Moses and Aaron prayed to God and that evening a flock of quails flew down and settled around the camp—and there was plenty for everyone. When dawn broke and the morning dew had disappeared, the earth was covered with white flakes, as fine as hoar frost, which they called 'Manna' or 'bread from heaven'. It tasted like a wafer made with honey. And from that time on until they reached the Promised Land, God sent Manna—a sufficient quantity for every day and a double portion on the sixth day so that the people could rest on the seventh day, the Sabbath, and keep it holy.

When another water shortage occurred, Moses was held personally to blame. By then they had reached Mount Horeb, where God had spoken to Moses from the burning bush. And here God spoke to him again: 'Moses, take your staff and I will show you where to strike it against a rock.'

Moses walked on ahead accompanied by a group of elders who watched in amazement as he struck the rock with his staff. At first a trickle and then a waterfall of cool, sparkling fresh water poured down the rock, enough and more for all that thirsty crowd.

The days of travelling turned into weeks and whenever there was a problem or a dispute within the community the people went to Moses or his brother Aaron who did their best to settle differences and never tired of teaching them to worship God. While they were camped at Mount Horeb, Jethro the Priest travelled from Midian to see his son-in-law. He rejoiced with Moses in everything that God had done for the Israelites. But he also showed concern. 'My dear son-in-law,' he said, 'you will soon wear yourself out with all your responsibilities. Even with your brother's help, it is impossible for one man to shoulder such a heavy burden. You must appoint groups of God-fearing, honest, capable men and give them the best training and instruction. These men,' he went on, 'will then be able to form permanent courts to hear and settle all but the most difficult disputes. In this way you will be relieved of the stresses and strains of leadership and preserve your strength to continue.'

When Jethro returned home, Moses acted on his father-in-law's sound advice, and the people became better organized and lived more in harmony.

They travelled on until they reached the great plain at the foot of Mount Sinai, where they pitched their tents. Then God spoke to Moses once more:

'I will give to my beloved Children of Israel, through you, a set of special Laws and Statutes which will govern their conduct every day of their lives, from birth to death.'

And Moses gave God's message to the people. Then he added, 'You are forbidden to go near Mount Sinai for it is God's most holy place. During the next two days prepare yourselves to receive God's commandments. On the third day you must be ready.'

As dawn broke on the third day the people assembled at the foot of the mountain—and waited.

The heavy silence was shattered by peals of thunder and flashes of lightning, as dense clouds and smoke covered the top of the mountain. And above all this, louder and louder, echoing round and round the mountain came the mighty blast of a thousand trumpets. The people were terrified and put their hands to their ears, trying to block out the deafening noise.

And then in the hush that followed, the people listened to God's ten important rules of behaviour:
'I am the Lord thy God who brought you out of Egypt.
Thou shalt not worship idols nor have any other God except Me.
Thou shalt not take the name of the Lord in vain.
Remember the Sabbath day and keep it holy.
Honour thy father and mother.
Thou shalt not kill.
Thou shalt not be unfaithful to husband or wife.
Thou shalt not steal.
Thou shalt not lie.
Thou shalt not covet other people's possessions.'

Then God asked Moses to go up through the black cloud to the top of the mountain. He stayed there for forty days, talking with God and listening to His teachings about His sacred laws. And God gave Moses two flat tablets of stone upon which He had written the Ten Commandments with his own hand.

Suddenly God was very angry: 'The children of Israel have broken their promises. They are offering sacrifices to an idol!' Then He thundered, 'For this I will destroy them!'

Afraid though he was, Moses spoke to God in defence of His people. 'They have broken their word because they are human and weak. But You are the Almighty God. Remember Abraham, Isaac and Jacob and the blessing You gave them.' And God relented and spared His people.

But Moses was not in a forgiving mood. He descended the mountain to face an appalling scene. Having become tired of waiting, the people had taken to drinking, dancing and brawling, and they were worshipping a golden calf! Moses stood there, too shocked to speak. And when they saw him standing on a rock holding the two tablets of stone, a deathly silence fell on the crowd.

Moses raised his arms and hurled the tablets with great force at the golden calf. They fell short and smashed to pieces. Then he destroyed the golden calf and went off alone, sad and discouraged.

The people were ashamed and afraid. They dreaded God's revenge, and the broken tablets only served to remind them of their disobedience. But God decided against punishment, and Moses was given another set of tablets. These, God said, were to be kept in a special chest known as the Ark of the Covenant and housed in a beautiful tent called the Tabernacle. It was to be made with many different materials—the best that could be found—to a specific measurement and design. And as long as the people wandered in the wilderness the Ark went with them. It was carried from place to place—a constant reminder of God's sacred rules for the way they should behave to Him and each other.

And the Children of Israel wandered in the wilderness for forty years until all those who had been born in slavery had died, and a new generation, born in freedom, was able to enter the Promised Land.

Not even Moses, and there has never been a prophet in Israel like him, before or since, was able to enter the Promised Land but God showed him a glimpse of the 'Land of Milk and Honey' from the top of Mount Nebo just before he died.

Heroes and heroines

The story of Samson is told in the Book of Judges in the Hebrew Bible. It takes place about the eleventh century before the Common Era, when the Hebrew people were under the rule of the Philistines. At that time the role of 'judges' was different from that of a judge today. Rather than trying cases in court, a judge was more a warrior and a leader in battle. Samson became a national hero for his lifelong fight against the Philistines and on one occasion he took on their army single handed. He was famous for his enormous strength and perhaps this was anticipated at his birth because his name Samson comes from a Hebrew word, *Shemesh* which means sun, man's source of strength and energy.

Long ago there was a man called Manoah, of the tribe of Dan, who lived in the town of Zorah in the lowlands of the Kingdom of Judah. To their great sorrow he and his wife were childless. They had always hoped and often prayed to God to bless them with a child and just when they were both finally resigned to their sad situation, an angel spoke to Manoah's wife:
'Your prayers to God have been answered, and soon you will give birth to a son. But listen carefully to everything I tell you. From now on you must not drink wine or any other strong drink, nor must you eat any forbidden foods. No one must ever cut the child's hair, for he is to become a Nazirite and will dedicate his life to the service of the Almighty God.'

Manoah and his wife wept for joy. Filled with gratitude, they killed a young goat and offered it, together with some grain, as a sacrifice to God.

Sure enough the angel's prophecy came true and the couple were blessed with a fine, strong, healthy baby son whom they called Samson. And Samson's mother obeyed all God's commands and prepared her son to become a Nazirite, a member of a holy Hebrew sect who made a special vow to God not to drink wine or cut their hair or beards.

By the time Samson was a young man he was easily recognizable by his great height, his good looks, his long hair and flowing beard. God had blessed him with tremendous physical strength but nevertheless he had one great weakness—he had a terrible temper which he found hard to control and which robbed him of common sense.

In those days the Kingdom of Judah was under Philistine rule, and there was no love lost between the occupying forces and the tribes of Israel. One day Samson went down to Timnath, in Philistine country. His parents did not approve of him visiting an enemy town, and when he returned and announced that he wanted to marry a young Philistine woman, they were upset and angry:
'Is there not one perfectly eligible young woman from among our own tribe, or all the other Hebrew tribes for that matter, that you must choose a stranger and a Philistine?' his mother protested. 'And remember you are a Nazirite,' Manoah added reproachfully. But Samson stubbornly ignored their remarks—his mind was made up.

On his way back to Timnath he had just reached the vineyards on the edge of the town when he heard a growling noise behind him. As he turned to look in the direction of the noise, he was taken wholly by surprise by a lion which sprang at him. Since he was unarmed, he used his bare hands to grapple with the animal and he tore it to pieces—as easily as if it had been a little goat. He left the lion's body under a clump of trees and continued his journey to see his betrothed: but he did not mention to her or anyone else his encounter with the hungry lion.

Samson returned home, and when the marriage plans had been agreed on, set out for Timnath once more, accompanied on this occasion by his parents. As they approached the vineyard he dropped behind in order to look at the place where he had killed the lion. By now the birds of prey had picked the carcass clean, but Samson noticed that a swarm of bees had made their home among its bones, and there was a good supply of honey as well. Moving with the utmost care so as not to disturb the bees, he managed to collect the honey, and carried some to his parents.

It was the custom in those days for a marriage ceremony to be followed by a wedding feast and general festivities which often lasted for a week. When the couple were married, the guests assembled to celebrate the joyous occasion. Samson, in festive mood, spoke to a group of young Philistine men who were his wife's kinsmen—thirty in all:
'I will tell you a riddle and I will give each of you a robe and a length of linen cloth for the correct answer. But if you fail you must give me the equivalent prize. What do you say?'

The men all agreed to the challenge, and Samson, recalling the lion and the honey said:
'Out of the eater came something to eat;
Out of the strong came something sweet.'

The riddle was greeted with laughter and everyone racked their brains and called out all kinds of answers—but not the right one. As the days wore on the contestants began to take the matter seriously. Not only was there an expensive prize at stake, but it became a question of pride for the Philistines. The last thing they wanted was to be made fools of in public. Tension ran high and tempers began to fray.

On the fourth day, when they were no nearer solving the puzzle the men were in an ugly mood. They went to see Samson's wife—in private.
'This stupid wager has gone far enough. We are, after all, your kinsmen and your wedding guests and we will not be ridiculed in this way any longer. Either you get the answer from your husband or we will burn down your father's house—with you in it!'

Samson's wife was terrified, for she realized that they would carry out their threat. Day after day she wept, wheedled, whined and pestered Samson for the answer.
'You have asked my kinsfolk a riddle and yet you have not told me—your wife—the answer,' she said.

Samson brushed the matter aside impatiently.
'I have told no one—not even my own mother and father, so why should I tell you?' he answered roughly.

But his wife was desperate and nagged him relentlessly. And on the seventh day, Samson finally gave in for the sake of peace, and told her how he had found the honey in the lion's carcass. And she went, in triumph, to tell the men.

And just before the festivities came to an end, the kinsmen answered Samson in unison: 'What is sweeter than honey? What is stronger than a lion?'

When Samson realized how he had been betrayed, a terrible rage came over him. In his madness he travelled to the city of Ashkelon and there killed several Philistine men. On his return, he kept his part of the bargain and handed robes and linen to the wedding guests. But they discovered the gifts had belonged to murdered men and fled in terror. Samson returned home, leaving his new bride behind.

The weeks passed and everyone was getting ready for the harvest. Samson was once more in control of his feelings and decided to visit his wife again. He took a young goat as a present and peace-offering for her.

His father-in-law greeted him politely but refused to allow him in: 'It seemed obvious to me from the way you treated my daughter and her kinsmen that you hated us all. And when you left her without a word I thought you had abandoned her. So I gave her in marriage to someone else—your groomsman.' He saw the look on Samson's face and added quickly 'But her sister is young and single—you are welcome to have her instead.'

Samson looked past his father-in-law to the fields beyond and walked away without a word—he was already plotting revenge. And this time it was arson—he set fire to the standing grain, the vineyards and the olive groves.

And from that time on things went from bad to worse. Surrounded by the devastation which Samson had caused, the Philistines burned his wife and her father as a reprisal.

So the people had cause to be terrified of Samson's violent temper—for it was as great as his physical strength, and wherever he went he left behind a trail of death and destruction. When at last he grew tired of taking such a terrible toll of human life, he escaped to a mountain cave.

Still the Philistines were bent on revenge and they decided to reach Samson indirectly through his own people. They gathered their army together but before the fight began, one of the leaders of the tribe of Judah protested, 'You have no cause to attack us—we have done nothing.'

And the Philistines replied, 'We want Samson for our prisoner—unless you capture him and hand him over the fighting will begin.'

So the men of Judah went to Samson and tried to reason with him.
'Whether we like it or not, we are a subject people under the rule of the Philistines. If you refuse to come with us, war will break out against us and the death of your own kinsmen will be forever on your conscience.'

Samson thought for a while, then got to his feet, towering over them all. 'Very well,' he told them, 'I agree to come with you on condition that you will not harm me, for your part of the agreement is simply to hand me over.'

The men of Judah readily agreed, and Samson allowed himself to be bound with strong ropes and led from the cave, down the mountain towards the Philistines waiting below.

Samson knew that he was in a dangerous situation. The men of Judah, having fulfilled their obligations, moved away. So now he stood alone, his arms tied down securely, facing the Philistine army, their weapons poised ready to kill him.

And then Samson felt God was with him and God gave him the strength to break the stout ropes. They snapped, one by one, like string. As soon as his hands were free, he looked round for a makeshift weapon. He found the whitened bone of an ass's jaw and once 'armed' he became a changed man.

The shouts of victory from the Philistines charging up the mountain towards him made him roar with fury. He ran straight at them, wielding the jawbone like an axe until the dead and dying lay thick on the ground. And the tale of Samson's strength was told and retold among the Hebrew people.

Time passed and Samson fell in love with a woman named Delilah, who came from the Valley of Sorek, near his home.

The Philistines never gave up hope that one day they would capture Samson and now they planned a new line of strategy: it all depended on Delilah.

'You have probably heard that we have an old score to settle with Samson,' one of the Philistine officers told her. 'Apart from being a giant with the strength of ten men, we think he is protected by some special means—perhaps magic or a god. All we ask of you is to find the secret of his strength and we will do the rest. For this information,' he added meaningfully, 'we will pay you handsomely.'

Delilah began a subtle and deceitful campaign of probing, gentle questioning, teasing and generally worming her way into Samson's confidence and affection. He was too infatuated to suspect her in any way but he grew tired of her persistence, and one day, in a weak moment, he told her his secret.
'I am a Nazirite,' he confided. 'We are a special people protected by God. No razor must ever touch my hair for every strand is my covenant with Him. If my hair was cut my promise to God would be broken and His protection would cease. All my strength comes from the Almighty.'

That was all Delilah needed to know. She cradled his head on her lap and lulled him into a deep sleep. Quickly and quietly she cut off his hair, and then called to the waiting men, who were able to overpower him.

The Philistines showed no mercy to their prize captive. They took him to the town of Gaza, blinded him, threw him in prison, bound him in iron chains, and worked him almost to death. They rejoiced in seeing his blindness, and whenever the mood took them they would taunt him. But while he was in prison Samson's hair began to grow again.

Some time later the Philistines planned a great celebration to offer sacrifices to their god, Dagon, for the safe capture of the man they had feared the most. It was held in a vast temple which was filled to capacity—several thousand people in all. They crowded into the main hall and even climbed up on to the flat roof. No one wanted to miss the Samson spectacle!

There were shouts from the crowd: 'Bring Samson here, and let us see if he can put up a good fight now!'

And a young guard was sent to bring him to the temple. As they approached Samson asked the boy: 'Place me where I can feel the pillars of the temple, so that I may lean against them.' And he prayed to God from the depths of his soul: 'Almighty God, remember me, please dear God, remember me. Give me back my strength just this once, and let me be avenged on the Philistines for taking away my sight.'

And God listened, and Samson put his left arm round one of the central pillars and his right arm round the other. Then he braced himself and pulled with all his strength. And the two tall columns cracked and then toppled, and with a mighty crash the entire building collapsed, killing Samson and everyone in it.

And so Samson, even in death, took vengeance on the enemies of Israel.

Susanna and the elders

The story of Susanna comes from the Apocrypha, a collection of Jewish writings composed between 200 BCE and 200 CE. It is important because it is the first example of a trial in which the witnesses were cross-examined separately to check their stories.

Long ago in Babylon there lived a wealthy Jew called Joakim. He was married to Susanna, a beautiful and devout woman who lived strictly according to the law of Moses.

Joakim held a prominent and influential position in the Jewish community. He owned a large house with a fine garden which became a regular meeting-place for elders and judges. The meetings took place in the morning so that by noon, when everyone had left for their midday meal, Susanna had the freedom and privacy to walk in her garden.

There were, however, two evil judges who had seen Susanna with her maids and, overwhelmed by her beauty, decided to accost her. The truth was that both were overcome with lust for her.

One hot day the two judges found her alone in the garden. It was the moment they had waited for and they sprang from their hiding place to confront her.

The first judge spoke to her. 'The garden

doors are shut and we are alone. If you refuse to do what we want, we shall say that we saw you here with a young man, and that you sent your maids away so you could be alone with him.'

In those days adultery was punishable by death and Susanna was appalled by the dreadful dilemma with which she was faced. But she stood proudly and spoke to the men with courage:

'I know that if I give in to you, I shall be killed, and I won't escape unharmed if I refuse. Either way I am doomed, but my choice in clear. It is better to reject you and face the consequences than sin before God.'

So before they could touch her, Susanna screamed loudly. The men rushed to open the garden gate and as soon as the servants came running out to investigate the disturbance, they were ready with their fabricated story.

The two judges, incensed by Susanna's refusal, were now determined on revenge. They insisted that she be brought before the community court and accused of adultery in front of her fellow Jews.

Susanna, like all modest women of the time was closely veiled. With quiet dignity she entered the room. There she had to suffer the dreadful humiliation of removing her veil to reveal her beautiful tear-stained face to the hostile gaze of the whole court.

In the silence that followed the two judges began their false accusations.

Susanna knew that her two wicked accusers would use their position to make their account seem plausible and she was right. When they described how they had found her alone in the garden with a young man, everyone in the room believed them and she was condemned to death.

As she was being led away, Susanna cried out, 'O Eternal, All-seeing God, from whom there are no secrets. You alone know that this evidence is false.'

Now a young man named Daniel was sitting in the front row and when he heard her anguished words, he leaped to his feet. 'Stop!' he shouted. 'I will not have this woman's death on my conscience.'

A ripple of curiosity ran through the room

and someone asked, 'What do you mean?'

'Listen to me, brother Israelites. Have you taken leave of your senses? Will you condemn a Jewish woman to death without proper investigation of the charge? I am sure these men are lying. The trial must be reopened!'

The people hurried back to reclaim their seats and a group of elders took Daniel to one side. 'With your permission, I believe I can prove the truth,' said Daniel. 'I am certain that these men are lying. We must separate them and examine them individually to see if their stories match.'

The elders were impressed by Daniel's suggestion and agreed to allow him to question the two judges. They were asked to leave the courtroom while Daniel addressed the assembly.

'Do not think for one moment that just because these men are elders and judges they are above abusing their positions of authority. If you will allow me, I shall now ask each of them the same question and you may all compare their answers.'

The first judge was brought in.

'What kind of tree were you standing under when you saw the couple together?' Daniel asked.

'It was an ash tree,' answered the judge.

'You are betrayed by your own lies—the angel of the Lord will burn you to a fine ash,' said Daniel fiercely, and he told the elders to take him away and fetch the second judge.

'Tell me, what kind of tree were you standing under when you saw them together?' asked Daniel.

'It was a clove tree,' said the second judge.

'Liar,' Daniel bellowed. 'The angel of the Lord stands with his drawn sword, waiting to cleave you in two.'

Then the crowd were on their feet shouting and cheering, praising God and thanking Daniel for seeing that justice was done. Everyone had heard the two judges' conflicting evidence: they had convicted themselves. The two men were punished in accordance with the law—with the same penalty they had planned for Susanna.

And she thanked God for His goodness and mercy and was happily reunited with her loving family.

The story of Ruth

The four short chapters of the Book of Ruth in the Hebrew Bible contain one of the most moving stories of devotion ever written. The events it describes took place in the land of Israel during the period of the Judges, in about the twelfth century BCE.

Many of the characters in the story appear to have names which describe their qualities. For example the translation of the Hebrew word Naomi is 'sweetness' and Ruth is 'friendship'. Mahlon is 'sickness' and Chillion is 'fading or wasting away'. The Hebrew name Orpah means the 'back of the neck', apparently to describe a person who turns away and leaves, while the name Boaz seems to indicate qualities of reliability and strength.

At the time when the story begins there was a drought in the land of Israel, crops were poor, work was difficult to obtain for the farm labourers and, more seriously, food was scarce.

Elimelech, his wife Naomi and their two sons Mahlon and Chillion decided to look elsewhere to find work and food. They left their home in Bethlehem and went to the country of Moab, situated to the east of the Dead Sea.

At first all went well. The family adjusted successfully to their life in new surroundings, the Moabite people were kind and friendly and work was plentiful. They lived well for a few years; and then everything changed.

Elimelech died suddenly and left Naomi sad and lonely. Despite her grief she cared deeply about her sons' future and wanted them to feel independent. In a typically unselfish manner she urged them to find partners of their own. She spoke quietly to Mahlon and Chillion: 'There is no need to worry about me. I can manage by myself. But you must think of yourselves, find suitable wives and settle down.'

The young men took their mother's good advice and married local Moabite young women. Mahlon, the elder son, married Ruth, and Orpah became Chillion's wife. Naomi found real pleasure in her new family. Her sons had chosen well and she came to love the young women as if they were her natural daughters.

They, in turn, had great affection for Naomi, and showed her all the love and respect due to a mother. But, alas, Naomi's happiness was short lived. A few years later Mahlon and Chillion both died, leaving their wives and their mother—three widowed women—sad, bereft, childless and alone in the world. After the funerals Naomi felt that once again the time had come for change. Apart from her deep regard for her daughters-in-law, there was nothing to keep her in Moab.

'I believe I must leave Moab and return to the land of Israel,' she told Ruth and Orpah. 'I need to spend my last remaining years among my own people. I have heard that the harvests there are good now, and food is plentiful, so I shall not go hungry. You know that I shall miss you both, but I hope in time you will consider remarrying and raising families of your own.'

The two women were distraught when they heard of Naomi's plans and implored her to stay. But when they saw her mind was made up, they ignored her advice in their desire to go with her.

Naomi was deeply affected but firm in her resolve. She repeated her counsel to her daughters-in-law—that they should find good husbands from among the local people. Orpah was eventually persuaded and, with tears in her eyes, she kissed Naomi and Ruth goodbye. But Ruth was different and stood her ground.

Naomi tried again. 'Look,' she said, 'your sister-in-law has returned to her own people and her gods and you should do the same.'

But Ruth was adamant. 'Naomi, I cannot stay here without you,' she said. 'I want to be with you wherever you go. You must not be concerned if there are questions asked about my being a foreigner, for I have made up my mind that your people will be my people and your God, my God.' And Ruth vowed that only death itself could part them. Naomi was too filled with emotion to speak. She embraced her faithful daughter-in-law and they travelled on together to Bethlehem.

As Naomi had predicted, they were able to settle down without difficulty as long as they lived frugally. Many friends remembered Naomi and her family and sympathized with

her tragic loss. But they were quick to see how fortunate she was to have such a faithful daughter-in-law, and Ruth the Moabitess's reputation became well-known in the neighbourhood. The people were full of admiration for the strong young woman who had adopted their ways and looked after Naomi with such loving care.

There lived in Bethlehem at that time a prosperous landowner, Boaz, a single man who was related to Naomi's late husband. Naomi mentioned this to Ruth and suggested that she might find work on his farm. 'The barley harvest has just started and it will be quite safe for you to go and glean in Boaz's fields,' Naomi told her. 'Our stock of barley meal is very low now,' she added ruefully. It was the custom among the Jews for the poor people to follow the reapers and gather up any stalks of grain they had left behind on the ground and Ruth joined the other women in the barleyfield.

Boaz was busy in the field supervising the reapers when he saw Ruth working with the gleaners. 'Who is that young woman?' he asked, and was told all about Ruth and the way in which she supported her widowed mother-in-law. At once he ordered his men to leave extra ears of barley for her to glean. He called Ruth over and spoke to her. 'I have heard how you have left your own people out of loyalty to Naomi. You are, indeed, a woman of worth and the Lord God will bless you for it,' he said. 'Come and glean here as often as you want; and if you sit with the women at midday you may rest assured that the men will not disturb you.'

When Ruth returned home that evening she told Naomi how kind and generous Boaz had been. She had managed to glean and thresh almost a bushel of barley meal, which pleased them both. From then on Ruth continued to glean in Boaz's field until the end of the harvest.

In those days Jewish law made it the responsibility of a close relative to marry a young widow for the sake of the dead kinsman. In that way she would be taken care of, her rights of inheritance secured, and the family name continued. Naomi explained the details. 'My late husband, Elimelech, owned a strip of land here. Had your husband, Mahlon, lived, he would have inherited it, but now he is dead you no longer have a right to it. I shall offer to sell it to Boaz for if he agrees to buy it, according to the law, he will also take you as his wife, and in that way you will have a claim on the land.' She looked at Ruth who was listening intently, and continued, 'Boaz is giving a feast to mark the end of the harvest. Go and ask his advice.'

Ruth changed her clothes and joined the labourers and gleaners at the harvest feast. Later, in her shy and modest way, she raised the matter with Boaz. He thought for a moment before answering, 'I am your servant, Ruth, and it will be my privilege to do whatever you ask. But are you quite sure I am the closest relative? I will make some enquiries for you.'

Boaz was as good as his word. He found out that there was, in fact, a relative nearer to the family than himself and he discussed the inheritance with him in the presence of ten witnesses chosen from among the elders of the community.
'When you purchase Naomi's field,' he told the man, 'you are bound by the law to take Ruth, the widow of Mahlon, the dead man's eldest son, for your wife, to perpetuate his name.' But the relative already had family responsibilities and could not agree for fear of endangering his own inheritance. So he instructed Boaz to act in his place and Boaz became the legal next-of-kin. As a sign that he was relinquishing his duty to Ruth's dead husband, the man, as was the custom, took off his sandal in the presence of the elders and handed it to Boaz.

With great love and pride, Boaz married Ruth, the Moabitess. They were blessed with a son Obed, much to the delight of his grandmother, Naomi, who derived great happiness and joy from him in her old age. And Obed became the grandfather of King David.

The festival of Shavuot—The Feast of Weeks, also known as the Feast of the Harvest—falls seven weeks after the spring festival of Passover. At this festival, the Book of Ruth is read in synagogues as a reminder of Ruth's loyalty and devotion, for its connection with the barley harvest and with King David, and because it commemorates the time when Moses received the Ten Commandments from God.

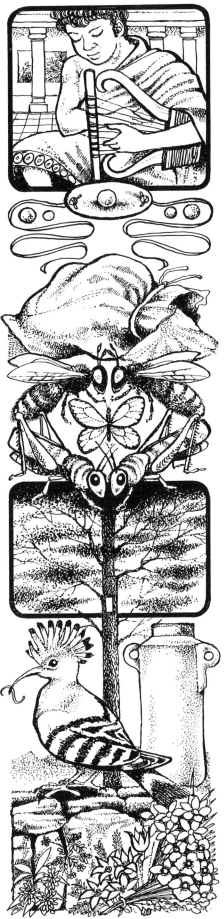

The kings

David, the son of Jesse and great-grandson of Ruth the Moabitess, rose from being a shepherd boy in Bethlehem to become King of Israel, which became a rich and powerful kingdom under his rule.

David was intelligent, handsome and protected by God. His name has been remembered by the Jewish people throughout the centuries as that of an almost ideal king, a legendary hero, a fine musician and a loyal servant of God. In folklore David is praised more for his poetic and musical ability and the fact that the Psalms of David were ascribed to him, than anything else—even more than for his heroic slaying of the giant Goliath. The two Books of Samuel, the First Book of Kings and the First Book of Chronicles tell of his great achievements and of the admiration the people held for him, even though it is made plain that he had several very human faults. It was David who established the city of Jerusalem as the capital of his kingdom, a holy city where the Ark of the Covenant, the sign of God's presence, could rest.

Solomon, King David's second son, succeeded his father as King of Israel and ruled for forty years from about 970 B C E. Although he was then only a young man of about twenty years old, he was aware of the great burden and responsibilities of kingship.

The Bible describes a dream in which God appeared to Solomon, saying: 'Tell me, what shall I give you?' Solomon answered, 'Though I am a mere child, unskilled in leadership, give your servant a mind with skill to listen, so that he may govern your people justly and distinguish good from evil.' God was so pleased that Solomon preferred wisdom above wealth and power that he granted his request and gave him honour and riches as well.

King Solomon became famous for his understanding and sound judgement and his reputation as a just ruler spread throughout the East. It was not only the Jewish people who valued King Solomon's leadership; people came from far and wide to listen and learn, to test him and to seek a just settlement in their disputes.

Because Solomon had placed such importance on gaining wisdom the folklore stories suggest that God had rewarded him with special powers, not only over people but also over angels, the dark world of spirits and demons, and over animals of all kinds. It was said that he

49

knew all their languages so that he could communicate with them and that he often used the eagle as his messenger.

The Temple which he built was reputed to have been the most beautiful structure in the world but, according to legend, Solomon's vanity and misconduct finally brought God's vengeance upon him. He was deprived of his power over people, demons, spirits, the animal kingdom and lastly over Israel itself, until all he had left was a beggar's staff. God appointed Ashmodai, the King of the Demons, to wear the crown of Israel in his place.

However as true repentance and a contrite heart are fundamental to religious belief among the Jewish people, King Solomon became worthy again after he had atoned for his sins.

The silent witnesses

Long, long ago when King Saul ruled over the Kingdom of Israel, a rich and lovely widow lived in the city of Ascalon. At that time the city was governed by Israel's enemies, the Philistines and one of the Philistine captains, an evil man, desired both the widow and her wealth for himself.

The widow was suspicious of the scheming captain. She did not want to marry him, nor give up the money left to her by her late husband. What could she do? One day while she was busy in her store-room she found the perfect answer. In those days large clay pots and jars were used for storage. She emptied her gold and silver shekels into several jars, filling them almost up to the neck. Carefully she filled the remaining space with thick honey which hid the treasure beneath. Next she asked her neighbour if he would take care of her honey jars while she was away. This he readily agreed to do. That same night the widow fled from the city to escape the clutches of the evil captain. In the meantime her neighbour hid the jars in his store-room.

Some time later the neighbour needed honey for his son's wedding feast and went to borrow some of the widow's, intending to return it later. It did not take him long to discover the hidden shekels and although he replaced the honey, he took the coins for himself.

Not long after this, the evil captain died and the widow returned to Ascalon. As soon as she arrived home she asked her neighbour for her jars of honey. When they were delivered she looked at them closely. Everything seemed to be in order and they were filled to the brim with honey, just as she had left them. But, alas, when she emptied the honey from one of the jars, to examine the coins beneath, she discovered that they had gone. From the weight of the other jars, she knew that each one was the same: all her savings had been stolen.

In despair she went to a judge and told him what had happened. He listened carefully, then asked, 'Did anyone see you put your gold and silver shekels in the jars?'

The poor widow shook her head.
'If you have no proof that you did as you say, there is nothing I can do,' the judge told her. 'Why don't you put this matter before the king and see if he can help?'

King Saul heard the widow's sad tale from beginning to end. But neither he nor his council of wise men could do anything. The widow knew that without proof her wicked neighbour would be able to keep all her money. She was so upset she sat down and began to weep.

The widow had not noticed a group of young boys playing nearby. One of them came up to her to ask what was the matter. The widow was touched by his kindness and poured out her whole sad story. 'Even the king and his counsellors cannot help me because there are no witnesses and no proof,' she sighed.
'Do not give up hope,' the young boy told her. 'Go back to King Saul and ask him if I may take up your case.'

So the widow returned to the king with the boy's request. Saul agreed to receive the boy and could hardly hide his astonishment when the young boy bowed before him.
'How can a mere boy like you solve this case, when wise judges have failed?' he asked.
'The case rests in God's hands, and I place my trust in Him,' the boy replied. King Saul then turned to the widow. 'Very well, go with the boy and let him help you if he can,' he said.

When they reached the widow's house, the boy looked closely at the jars of honey. Then he called in the neighbour and his friends and asked, 'Are these the widow's jars which you stored for her?' The neighbour nodded in reply.

Next the boy asked the servants to empty all the honey into other pots. Then, one by one, he smashed all the empty jars and held them up so that everyone could see inside them. Suddenly they saw two shining silver shekels which had remained stuck to the side of one of the jars, well out of reach of the thief. The boy held up the shekels and, turning to the widow, said: 'Here are two silent witnesses to prove your neighbour's guilt!'

There was no arguing now. The neighbour confessed and returned all the stolen money to the widow.

King Saul and all Israel marvelled when they heard how the young boy's wisdom had saved the widow and they knew that the spirit of God was with him.

The name of the young boy was David.

David and Goliath

When David was a young shepherd boy, Israel was frequently engaged in border warfare against the Philistines. On one occasion the two armies were preparing for battle on opposite sides of the valley of Elah. Although David was too young to enlist, he was well aware of the effects of a nation at war because his three elder brothers were already serving in King Saul's army.

One day David's father, Jesse, sent him from their home in Bethlehem to the battle front for news of his brothers. No sooner had he arrived in the camp than David witnessed an extraordinary scene. On the other side of the valley, where the Philistines had pitched their tents, David saw a giant of a man carrying an enormous spear and encased in armour from head to foot. He stood there, like a tall tower in silhouette, and bellowed, 'I am Goliath from the city of Gath. I challenge one of Saul's men to meet me in a fair combat. If I kill him, your army will submit to us, and if he kills me, the

Philistines will surrender. What, are you an army of cringing cowards that you cannot find a volunteer?' And the taunts and jeers continued to echo across the valley.

The situation looked bleak. The hard facts had to be faced. There was no one on Israel's side, from King Saul himself, down through the ranks, who could match Goliath either in size, strength or in the skills of combat. At that time the Israelite army was composed of simple men—farmers and shepherds like David himself—who were given only primitive military training and the crudest of weapons with which to defend themselves. Everyone had come to dread the giant Philistine's daily insults, and morale was at its lowest.

David was furious to see the effect Goliath had on Saul's men. When he met his brothers he burst out, 'Why do you allow the enemy to provoke our God-fearing men? Why doesn't someone go out and kill him and silence him forever?'

David's eldest brother Eliab did not take kindly to these cutting remarks. 'You had no business to leave the family's flocks, in fact you are much too young to be here at all. Take my advice, and do not interfere in matters which do not concern you,' he snapped. 'Now get off home and remember to give our greetings to Father.'

But David ignored his brother's scathing reply. His mind was full of plans for putting an end to Goliath's boasting once and for all. He spoke quietly to Eliab. 'Take me to King Saul. I wish to tell him that I have made up my mind to accept the Philistine's challenge.'

Eliab opened his mouth to rebuke David but quickly closed it again. One look at the expression on his young brother's face was enough to convince him that he was in deadly earnest.

Saul was touched by David's offer to take up Goliath's challenge but warned him against the idea.
'I am grateful for your patriotic gesture but I cannot accept it. Goliath is a fully trained soldier—a war veteran of long standing. The skills you require to be a good shepherd will be of little use against such a man.'

David was not to be dissuaded. 'I am no stranger to dangerous situations,' he argued, 'and I have often been attacked by wild animals. I have even killed lions and bears to protect my flock. I have always put my trust in God and he has saved my life on more than one occasion. I have no doubt He will help me now.'

Saul was deeply moved by the force of David's argument and reluctantly agreed to let him go. 'Go then if you must and may the Almighty God be with you,' he said. And when he had blessed David he gave him his own helmet, his coat of mail and his sword.

David thanked Saul and replied, 'My Lord King, do not be offended if I choose not to wear your armour. The weight of the helmet and coat will only hamper my movements.' Then he smiled and said, 'As for your sword, I can barely lift it, let alone wield it!' And he left the king, to prepare for the battle in his own way.

David had devised a simple but clever plan. He would need a clear head, a quick eye, a true aim, and more importantly, the spirit of God within him. For David planned to make the Philistine drop his guard when confronted by a mere shepherd boy, apparently unarmed except

for his staff. He would keep a good distance between them—out of reach of Goliath's sword and spear—and then attack him with a completely unexpected weapon, for which the Philistine would be totally unprepared.

David made sure that his sling was in full working order and, unnoticed by the others, he went down to a little brook and selected five smooth stones which he put in his pouch. He carefully hid the pouch and the sling under his coat. Then, with a fervent prayer to God, young David was ready for the fight.

Goliath, head and shoulders taller than anyone else in the Philistine army, marched out, preceded by his shield bearer. He stared in astonishment at the young boy walking towards him armed only with a shepherd's staff. He boiled with fury and contempt.
'Is this Israel's only contestant?' he shouted mockingly at David. 'Is there not one single soldier in King Saul's army to match a Philistine warrior? Am I a dog that this boy comes to me with a staff? When I have killed him his dead body will make good pickings for the birds and beasts.' And he cursed David by the gods of his people.

And David answered: 'You are armed with a sword, spear and shield but I am protected by the Almighty God—the God of Israel. I will kill you in His name and put the Philistine army to flight.'

And with that David ran towards Goliath. When he judged he was at the right distance from his target, he dropped his staff, loaded his sling, took aim and hurled one of the stones with all his strength. The stone struck the Philistine's forehead with such deadly force and accuracy that he fell unconscious to the ground. Before anyone had realized properly what had happened, David ran forward, drew out Goliath's sword and used it to cut off his head.

And then a mighty roar of victory rang across the valley from King Saul's men. The Philistine army was helpless without their champion and the Israelites pursued the fleeing enemy until the battle was decisively won.

From that moment David became the hero of Israel, a hero who was later destined to become their king.

The old woman and the wind

Long, long ago an old woman came to Jerusalem to see the wise King Solomon. 'Please, Your Majesty, will you punish the wicked wind who is my life-long enemy?' she asked.

The king was puzzled by such a strange request. 'Did you say the wind? How can the wind be your enemy?' he said.

The old woman sighed. 'Listen to my story and then you will understand,' she said. 'I am a poor widow and lived in a wooden hut by the sea. Although it was old and rickety it gave me shelter. I earned an honest living from weaving and repairing the fishermen's nets. One day there was a terrible storm and fierce winds lashed the waves as high as mountains. Day after day the wind howled and shrieked. The sea was too rough for the fishermen to take their boats out, and I had no work when their nets were not being used. No work and no money to buy flour. My stock became smaller and smaller until there was not enough flour left to bake one last loaf of bread.

'I was forced to go to the fields after the harvest had been gathered in. There I picked up the grain the reapers had left behind. It was back-breaking work, bending down from morning to night. I blamed the wind for that miserable job—scratching the earth all day for no more than a handful of barley. I was so tired and hungry that I burst out crying. Maybe the good Lord took pity on me then for the farmer gave me some of his own grain. I took his gift and my own gleanings and ground them into a few pounds of flour. I tied it up carefully in my headscarf and, pushing hard against the wind, I went home.

Not far down the road I met a man staggering along. He stopped in front of me and moaned: "Please help me. A terrible fire has spread through my village burning everything—every home, every animal and. . ." The poor man stopped for a moment, quite speechless with emotion. "Every man, woman and child. I was the only one who managed to escape alive. I am starving, have you any food to spare?" I took pity on the poor man and gave him half my flour. Then I thanked God that I was able to help him just as the farmer had helped me.

'It was a tiring journey but I arrived home at last. Then as I lifted the latch of the door, a sudden violent gust of wind blew me off my feet and snatched the bag of flour out of my hand. I got up and ran after it as fast as I could, but it was no use. The bag blew up and down, and this way and that, then it was tossed out to sea and out of sight. Gasping for breath, I hurried back to my hut. Imagine my horror when I saw it had been blown down. All that was left was a pile of broken wood. My strength had gone. I slumped to the ground too weak to move.'

She paused, then added, 'Perhaps you can understand now why I beg you, wise king, to punish the wind and right my wrong.'

The king and his counsellors were moved by the good woman's misfortunes. She was given bread and wine and a place to rest while the king thought the matter over.

Meanwhile three strangers had arrived at the palace and were waiting outside to see King Solomon. They each had a big sack strapped onto a donkey. When they were brought before the king they bowed and said, 'We are merchants who met by chance. We hired a boat to carry our goods back to our own land. Sacks of silver and gold we had, priceless jewels and the finest spices. We had only been at sea a short time when we were caught in a sudden storm. The force of the wind whipped up the waves until they towered above us. We were tossed about like a cork on the water, and the boat's timbers creaked and groaned under the strain. Suddenly we saw that the sea had burst through a hole in the bottom of the boat. Frantically we tried to stop the hole with anything we could find, but nothing worked. The boat was filling with water and we knew we would soon be drowned. We shouted for help to many strange gods, but all for nothing. Finally we prayed to the God of Israel, vowing to exchange all our goods for our lives. Then the strangest thing happened. A kind of bundle appeared out of the sky, dropped into the hole like a plug and blocked it up. At the same

moment the wind died down and the sea became calm. We were saved! We rowed hard to the nearest port and took the shortest route to Jerusalem. Now we would like to keep our promise and give our treasures in thanksgiving to the God of Israel.'

King Solomon listened carefully and then asked, 'Did you see what was inside the bundle?'

'It was only a small bag of flour,' one of the merchants replied. 'We kept it to remind us of how it had saved our lives.' And he placed a little bag of flour in front of the king.

The king sent for the old woman, who could hardly believe her eyes when she saw it. 'Why this is mine,' she said. 'It is the bag of flour the wind snatched from me.'

King Solomon smiled and spoke to the merchants. 'Give your treasures to this woman for she has a right to them. The truth is that although God saved you from drowning, this woman was his messenger.'

And turning to the old woman he said, 'Take these sacks of silver and gold and jewels as a reward for saving the lives of these men.'

To the king's surprise the old woman shook her head. 'I cannot take the treasure,' she said. 'It was meant as a thanksgiving gift for God's Holy Temple, not for me. I am a working woman and all I need are the tools of my trade to earn an honest living.'

The old woman's words so impressed the king that he gave her a room in his palace where she lived in peace and comfort. There she forgot all about the wind and the sea and spent her days weaving beautiful cloth to hang in the Holy Temple in Jerusalem.

The little bee

One hot day King Solomon settled himself comfortably under a fig tree to take his afternoon sleep. His servants stood quietly at his side. Carefully they waved large fans slowly backwards and forwards to cool him and keep away the flies.

He had just nodded off to sleep when a little bee suddenly darted between the fans, landed on the king's nose and stung him. The painful sting woke him with a start and made him very angry. And no wonder! His nose was not only sore and swollen but beginning to turn red.

The king was determined to punish the impudent creature who had dared to hurt him. Vowing revenge, he joined his servants in a search to find the little bee. But she had seen the king's bad temper and had flown for her life. 'I will find the culprit!' King Solomon roared, clutching his painful nose and he ordered every bee, hornet, wasp and ant, in fact every kind of insect in his kingdom to assemble before him. The news spread quickly to the insect world. Soon a great fluttering and fussing, swooping and swarming began. From nests, trees, flowers and bushes, clouds of insects rose and landed before the king. They buzzed about in panic and confusion, trying to discover the reason for the king's command. 'Buzzzz. . .what is the matter? Why has the king sent for us?'

By this time the king's nose was the size and colour of a tomato. Smarting with pain and anger he stamped his foot and shouted, 'Silence!'

The crowd of insects fell silent. Not a wing stirred, not a cricket chirped, not a bee buzzed.

Pointing to his nose, King Solomon bellowed, 'Who has done such a wicked thing to the king?'

Gradually a murmur spread from swarm to swarm, echoing the king's question. 'Buzzzz. . .who has done such a wicked thing to the king?'

Then everything went quiet again as one little bee rose up from the crowd and flew straight to King Solomon.

'It was I, your Majesty. I was the one.'

'You,' roared the king at the top of his voice. 'Have you no respect for the king's nose or fear of the king's anger?'

The little bee trembled but she went on, 'Do not be angry, Your Majesty. It was a foolish mistake and I am very sorry. I am only a young bee and have not yet learned to tell the difference between a flower and a nose—especially the king's nose!'

Solomon was impressed by the little bee's brave defence and for one brief moment it looked as if he was going to smile. But the pain of the sting soon reminded him of his bad mood.

'And what have you to say for yourself?' he thundered. The little bee summoned all her courage and answered.

'Your Majesty is wise and forgiving. Please spare my life so that when you need me, I can repay your kindness and be of service to you.' This time there was no holding back. The king burst out laughing.

'Well,' he said, 'the very idea—that a bee can be of service to the king! Be off with you before I . . .' But the little bee had spread her wings and was gone before the king could finish.

The more the king thought of the little bee repaying his kindness the more he laughed. And in his good humour he forgave the other bees, too, and sent them and all the other insects away in peace. In the meantime the royal doctors prescribed healing ointment for the painful sting. By the time the swelling had gone down the king had forgotten all about the matter.

Now the Queen of Sheba had heard of King Solomon's wisdom and travelled from her own country to visit him. She arrived with her attendants, who carried many costly gifts for the king. The queen enjoyed testing wise King Solomon with all kinds of puzzles and problems and difficult questions. But try as she might, with all her cunning and riddles, the king was able to solve them all. At last the queen devised a puzzle that she was sure would defeat him. She ordered her attendants to bring bouquets of artificial flowers, all but one bouquet so skilfully made by the queen's finest craftsmen that no one could tell them from real, living flowers. Then she ordered the attendants to come before the king. Somewhere among the mass of bright colours was a single bouquet freshly picked from the palace gardens.

When everything was ready the queen asked Solomon, 'Tell me, O wise king, which are the living flowers and which are those that have been made by hand?'

The king peered at each bouquet closely, examining them from every side, but it was no use: he could not tell them apart.

'The queen will have the better of me this time,' he thought bitterly.

Whilst the king was hesitating, not knowing quite what to do next, he heard a faint buzzing near his ear. It was the little bee!

'Watch me,' she whispered and flew without hesitation straight to the bunch of fresh flowers.

The king smiled. The Queen of Sheba and all her household were amazed when he pointed confidently to the bouquet on which the bee had settled. 'This is the bunch of living flowers,' he said.

So the little bee was, after all, able to be of service to the king.

A match made in heaven

While the Queen of Sheba was visiting King Solomon in Jerusalem, the king never tired of regaling her with the wonders of God and the queen listened enthralled to descriptions of His great miracles. One day King Solomon was explaining to her how marriages were arranged by God in heaven, even though each match was as difficult to make as it had been for Him to part the Red Sea.

'I believe everything you have told me about your great and wonderful God,' the queen interrupted, 'but this I cannot understand. Tell me how is it possible for Him to make marriages in heaven? With your permission, I would like to put this matter to the test.'

King Solomon knew full well how much the queen liked to test his faith and wisdom and he asked how she would proceed.

'My plan is this,' the queen explained. 'I suggest we walk through the streets of Jerusalem and I shall choose an unmarried maiden whom you will arrange to send away to a deserted island. As soon as she lands she is to be imprisoned at the top of a tall tree. There she will be totally isolated. That, I think, should prove to be a fair test of whether or not your God can provide a match for her.'

King Solomon readily agreed and they went together to look for a suitable maiden.

It was a busy time of day and the king and queen soon found themselves among jostling crowds. They saw many young girls but the queen, careful in her observations, was not yet ready to make a selection. However, once they had left the noisy market behind she noticed a beautiful girl drawing water from a well. 'That is the one,' she said. 'Let us see what will happen to her when she has to live in a tree on an island for five long years. I wonder how your God will make a match for her there!'

The young girl, whose name was Penina, was overcome with embarrassment when she recognized King Solomon and the Queen of Sheba, and quite startled when they asked to meet her mother and father. The king told her parents that he wished to employ their daughter for five years and offered them a substantial sum of money in compensation, which they gratefully accepted.

When Penina learned how she was to spend the next five years, she was heartbroken. However, she knew it would be useless to protest and decided there and then to bear her future solitude as best she could.

So the unhappy girl was taken to a distant island, completely cut off from all human contact. A huge old tree grew in the forest there and a small room was hollowed out of its trunk for her to live in. It had one door, locked from the outside, and a window large enough for all necessities to be passed through but too small for her to escape. The room was furnished simply, and there were musical instruments and a loom to help while away the time. And so Penina tried to fill her lonely days weaving beautiful cloth, singing sweet songs and playing on the musical instruments. Since King Solomon knew the language of the birds, he entrusted a magic pheasant to guard her and to provide for all her needs.

About this time a ship was on its way to the Holy Land. While the captain was resting below, his young son, Reuben, took over the steering wheel. All went well for a time and the ship made good headway but suddenly a fierce storm blew up. The wind filled the sails and the angry waves tossed the boat about like a toy. A towering wave crashed onto the deck, sweeping Reuben and several of the sailors overboard. Luckily Reuben managed to cling on to a plank of wood which was floating nearby. Although he was weary almost to the point of death, he hung on grimly until he was washed ashore on an island many miles from his father's ship.

After the storm had abated the captain spent days searching the sea for survivors, especially for his beloved son. He blamed himself for his terrible loss, for he believed that had he been on deck when the storm struck, he might have been able to steer the ship to safety. Eventually he called off the search and sailed on.

Although Reuben was still weak and exhausted from his ordeal, he decided to explore the island. All he had left in the world were the clothes he wore and a knife. But he was able to sustain himself with fruit and nuts.

The island was small and in his daily quest for food Reuben soon came across a great tree that towered over all the others. He was just wondering how best he might scale it to pick its fruit when he saw a most extraordinary sight. High above him a pheasant circled round with a basket in its beak. The bird perched on a branch and carefully passed the basket through a little window in the side of the tree. Something—he could not see what—took the pheasant's offering and disappeared from view.

Reuben could hardly believe his eyes. He determined to discover who or what was hidden in the tree. For several days he watched the pheasant to chart the times of its arrival and then, when it was safe, he climbed up to the little window. To his surprise a beautiful young girl looked back at him.

Reuben shouted to her. Penina was frightened by the sound of a human voice. 'Who is there?' she called timidly. 'I was washed overboard in a storm and marooned on this island. But who are you?' Reuben asked.

Then Penina poured out her sad story. Reuben was amazed at all he heard and settled down on a branch near the little window where the two young people could see each other. They continued to talk far into the night. And when the sun rose the following morning they were still deep in conversation. By this time neither had any doubts about the love and affinity they shared.

Then, taking his knife, Reuben cut away the vines from around the window and patiently carved away at its frame until the opening was large enough for him to climb inside.

The next day when the pheasant arrived with its daily ration of food for Penina, it saw Reuben in the room with her. Swiftly it flew back to King Solomon with the news. He was delighted but decided to await natural developments before he told the Queen of Sheba. He ordered the pheasant to provide sufficient food for the two young people and sent the finest delicacies from his royal kitchen.

As the young couple's love for each other flourished and grew they decided to get married and the magic pheasant provided a sumptuous wedding feast to which all the creatures of the forest were invited.

A year later the couple were blessed with a lovely baby daughter whom they named Sheba, after the queen who had, unknowingly, brought them together. For Penina and Reuben realized that had it not been for the queen's wager, they might never have met. The pheasant at once reported the good news to the king, who began to think that it was high time he told the Queen of Sheba about the match.

Shortly after this happy event, King Solomon's son was to be married and invitations were sent out to royal families and notables of the highest rank. The Queen of Sheba was among the invited guests and the king decided to use the occasion to end Penina and Reuben's lonely exile. A ship was sent to carry them to the royal wedding.

Once the couple reached land the magic pheasant guided them towards Jerusalem. From time to time they rested and at each well where they stopped to drink, Reuben noticed a portrait of a young man, cleverly positioned to catch the eye of any passing traveller. Reuben, who had learned the language of the birds during his time in the tree house, asked the pheasant if the picture represented a god whom the local inhabitants worshipped.

'No,' answered the pheasant. 'It is not an idol. This is the land of Israel and the people here recognize one God, the Almighty God. A sea captain whose son was swept overboard placed his picture at every stopping place in the hope that someone somewhere might recognize him and reunite him with his grieving father.'

Tears streamed down Reuben's cheeks when the pheasant had finished speaking.

'I am that captain's son,' he said. 'I was saved by floating wreckage and landed on the island where Penina was imprisoned. I wonder where my father is now.'

They continued on their journey to Jerusalem and when they arrived at the palace, Penina explained Reuben's story.

'This is indeed a day of celebration,' said the king and he sent messengers to bring the captain, and Penina's parents, to join in the wedding festivities. It was the happiest and most joyful of reunions.

As for the Queen of Sheba, she was able to witness for herself how the Holy One had blessed Penina and, how, despite all obstacles, He had joined her with the man she was destined to marry. Here was the proof that marriages are made in heaven and she never doubted the word of King Solomon again.

King Solomon and the shamir

More than anything else King Solomon dreamed of building a temple to the glory of the God of Israel. Each time he thought about it a particular sentence from the Book of Exodus came into his mind: 'If you make me an altar, you must not build it of hewn stones, for if you use a chisel on it, you will profane it.' Solomon knew the meaning of this verse. Whereas the altar and the temple were symbols of life and peace, the chisel and other metal tools represented the sword—an instrument of war and death. But how could a temple of stone be built without the use of metal implements? There seemed to be no way of carrying out God's sacred instructions.

Thus it was that the wisest of monarchs had no idea how to begin his difficult task, let alone complete it. Yet everything was in place. Great cedar trees had been brought from Lebanon and there were vast quantities of marble and granite in store. But how could these great blocks of stone be split and giant trees be sawn up without the use of tools?

He sought advice from his wisest counsellors but not even their great knowledge of the Holy Scriptures could help. Then one of the most deeply respected of the sages approached him. 'My Lord King,' he said, 'with respect, may I remind you that among God's countless creatures there is a tiny but wonderful animal—a miraculous worm called the shamir. It is said to be one of the ten marvels created by the Almighty on the eve of the first Sabbath day. Although it is no bigger than a grain of barley the shamir can split stone better than the sharpest iron tool.'

King Solomon was delighted to hear this. 'Tell me, learned counsellor, where may I find this miraculous worm?' he asked.
'I am sorry to say that no man knows its whereabouts,' the counsellor replied. 'But as God has bestowed upon Your Majesty a deep insight into birds, beasts, demons and spirits perhaps they can help you now.' Solomon was grateful for this wise counsel and lost no time in putting it to good use.

The king wore a gold ring on which was inscribed God's Divine Name. As soon as he had pronounced it a demon appeared before him. Bowing low, the demon asked: 'What is your wish, Solomon, King of Israel?'
'Tell me where I can find the shamir,' the king ordered.

The demon trembled. 'Alas, I cannot help you, O king of men and spirits. Only Ashmodai, the King of the Demons, knows where the shamir can be found.'
'And where can I find Ashmodai?'
'He lives far away on top of a mountain,' replied the demon nervously. 'During the day he goes about his duties, flying to heaven for orders and from there to every corner of the earth. When he returns at night he goes straight to a well which supplies his drinking water. It is kept tightly sealed by an enormous rock and only when Ashmodai is sure that the seal has not been broken does he quench his thirst.'

King Solomon listened intently and a plan began to take shape in his mind. When the demon had gone he sent for his trusted captain, Benaiah. 'Benaiah, my friend, do what I tell you, capture Ashmodai, the King of the Demons, and bring him to me. Take this and wear it.' And the king gave Benaiah a golden chain. 'The letters of God's Holy Name are engraved on each link,' he explained. He then took off his ring. 'Take great care of my ring for it is inscribed with the Almighty's name. These are my treasured possessions and will protect you at all times.' Then King Solomon explained to Benaiah exactly what he must do.

Benaiah made all the necessary arrangements for his journey. He packed food, tools, chains, several jars of strong wine and a fleece of wool. When everything was ready he asked Solomon for his blessing and set off, with his men, to find the King of the Demons.

It took many days to reach the foot of the mountain and several more to climb up to Ashmodai's home. Early one morning Benaiah at last found the well and used the rest of the day to carry out the king's orders. He set his men to dig a pit immediately below the well. Then they made an underground channel so that the water from the well could flow into the pit. When the well was emptied, the hole to the channel was plugged with wool. Then a second pit was dug out above the level of the well, with a second channel leading from it down into the side of the well. Finally the jars of wine were emptied into the higher pit and the wine flowed freely into the well below. Everything was working according to plan. The well water had been changed to wine and the seal to the well remained unbroken. When all traces of their work had been carefully concealed, Benaiah and his men hid out of sight, anxiously awaiting the approach of the King of the Demons.

They had good reason to be frightened. With a mighty roar of thunder the heavens seemed to split open as Ashmodai appeared. He was a huge and terrible creature, part man, part animal, breathing fire from his nostrils. He made straight for the well and scrutinized the seal for any signs of disturbance. Then he rolled the huge stone away with a single movement of his hand.

Ashmodai leaned over to scoop out some water, only to be almost overpowered by the heady fragrance of strong wine. 'Who has been tampering with my water?' he bellowed angrily. 'Who has put wine in my well? Wine is a curse—it destroys reason and dulls the senses and I will not drink it.' Ashmodai stormed and raged but at last his thirst got the better of him and he swallowed so much wine that he crashed to the ground in a drunken stupor.

This was the moment Benaiah had been waiting for. Quickly and quietly he crept up to Ashmodai, bound him with chains, placed the king's golden chain around his neck and sealed it with the royal ring.

Some hours later, when the effects of the wine were beginning to wear off, Ashmodai awoke. He strained every sinew in his body to break the fetters. Sparks of fire flew from his eyes and he screamed at Benaiah: 'Is it you who have bewitched me?'

Benaiah replied, 'I have acted on the orders of my master, King Solomon. It is useless to try and escape for the chain bears the seal of God.' At the sound of these words Ashmodai knew the fight was over and he gave in to his captor without further struggle.

After a long and difficult journey Benaiah brought the King of the Demons to the Holy City of Jerusalem. As soon as Ashmodai saw King Solomon he took his staff, drew a rectangle on the floor with it and flung the staff at the king's feet.
'What is the meaning of this?' asked the king.
'You may be the most powerful king on earth,' Ashmodai thundered, 'but when you die you will be buried in a plot of earth this size,' and he pointed to the shape he had drawn. 'Are you not satisfied with all your human subjects, that you strive to conquer spirits and demons as well?'
'I have no wish to triumph for its own sake,' Solomon said. 'You were brought to Jerusalem for a worthy cause. I wish to build a temple to the glory of God, and for this purpose I need the wonderful worm shamir to split the stones. Tell me, Ashmodai, where can I find this creature?'

Ashmodai answered calmly, 'The shamir was given to Rahab the Prince of the Sea. He in turn entrusted it to the hoopoe bird who uses it to transform the bare wilderness. First she places the shamir on top of a rock, which immediately splits beneath it. Then the hoopoe drops the seeds of all kinds of plants, shrubs and trees into the crevices. In time the seeds take root and cover the barren earth with life-giving foliage. The bird nests in a cave on top of a sheer cliff. She keeps the shamir in a secret place nearby.'

Once more the king gave Benaiah instructions and his blessing and Benaiah and his men left Jerusalem for the desert where the hoopoe bird lived. After many weary months they came to the cave Ashmodai had described, and, inside it, found the hoopoe's nest.

The nest was full of hungry, gaping fledglings waiting for their mother to return with food. Immediately Benaiah ordered his men to block the cave mouth with a boulder. Then they hid to await the bird's return. Soon they heard the sound of flapping wings and she landed in front of the cave with her beak full of food. She could hear her helpless chicks calling but was quite unable to reach them. She dropped the food and pecked at the rock time and time again. Watching carefully from his hiding place, Benaiah saw the hoopoe fly off again. When she returned she was carrying the shamir in her beak. Still holding the little worm by its tail, she placed it on the stone—and the stone shattered instantly.

Shouting and banging, Benaiah and his men leaped out. The noise startled the bird, she dropped the shamir and Benaiah picked it up and put it in a box.

There was great rejoicing when Benaiah returned to Jerusalem with the shamir. The wonderful little creature split the great stones for the king so that the work of building a temple was soon under way. And during the next seven years no one ever heard the banging of hammers nor the tapping of chisels or any other metal tools. Everything was done according to the law of Israel and in a manner pleasing to God. Solomon's dream was fulfilled at last when he dedicated the magnificent temple to the glory of God. As soon as the solemn service was over the shamir disappeared—for ever.

The prophets

In biblical times, a prophet was not simply someone who foretold the future. Instead, he was a man of unusual powers and gifts who was inspired by God to guide and teach the people, to explain His ways and interpret messages from God to the Children of Israel. The people of Israel were surrounded by other tribes who worshipped different gods and the prophets constantly warned against idol worship, only foretelling the future in the sense that they 'prophesied' disaster for those who ignored their warnings. The prophets were like elder statesmen—they advised kings as well as ordinary people and were usually treated with great respect.

Moses was the first of these great figures who shaped the religious faith of the Children of Israel and he became the finest example for all future prophets. With God's help Moses led the Israelites out of slavery in Egypt and he never let them forget that their escape was due to God's help. Later, when the Israelites had settled in the land of Canaan, the prophet Samuel was guided by God to choose a king, to unite the people against their common enemy, the Philistines.

Elijah lived later, in the ninth century before the Common Era when the Israelites had forgotten their true religion and begun to worship Baal—a false god. Elijah brought them back to the worship of one God.

In the eighth century before the Common Era there were four great prophets whose teachings can still be read in the Hebrew Bible: Amos, Hosea, Isaiah and Micah. Once again, the people of Israel had fallen into evil ways. Each of the four prophets had his own particular message, but they all warned that nothing but disaster would come to nations that ignored the laws of God.

When the prophets' warnings were fulfilled, and Jerusalem was conquered by the Babylonians in 586 B C E the temple was destroyed and the leaders of the Jews were driven into exile. One of the greatest of the Hebrew prophets, Isaiah, inspired the people with a message of hope, prophesying that the Jews would one day be able to return to the Holy Land and rebuild their shattered city. In 538 B C E Isaiah's prophecies were fulfilled and the exiled Jews were allowed to return to their land.

Elijah the prophet

The stories of the prophets Elijah and his successor Elisha are written in the two Books of Kings in the Hebrew Bible. The biblical account describes how the Israelites had begun to worship the pagan god Baal and Elijah's tireless efforts in helping them restore their faith in the true God. Elisha continued his work after his death.

At the time when Elijah was alive, Israel was divided into two, the Kingdom of Israel in the north, and the Kingdom of Judah in the south. They were bitter rivals and sworn enemies, and to make matters worse, religious, social and political corruption was rife throughout the north. It was clear to Elijah that this situation could not last.

To make matters worse, the Kingdom of Israel was ruled by Ahab, a weak king, and his wicked wife Jezebel, who exerted an evil influence on her husband. The Bible tells that Ahab did more wrong in the eyes of the Lord than all his predecessors put together. He introduced the worship of Baal, and made no attempt to restrain Jezebel from spreading a deep hatred of God's prophets.

Elijah, who came from Tishbe in Gilead, and was known as Elijah the Tishbite, confronted Ahab with a dire warning that unless he gave up idol worship, God would send a severe drought as a punishment. The drought came and God told Elijah to go into the wilderness; while the country suffered, God sent ravens to feed him.

As the drought continued, Ahab accepted a trial proposed by Elijah to prove to the people who was the true God. Two altars were built on Mount Carmel and a bull sacrifice was prepared for each of them. The wood fires were ready but not kindled. Hundreds of Baal-worshipping priests prayed to Baal for fire but none came, whereas when Elijah prayed God sent fire to burn the sacrifice. As the smoke from the sacrifice rose into the sky, the rain began to fall, and the drought came to an end. The people had witnessed for themselves the miraculous sign from God and they turned on the pagan priests and rejected the worship of Baal.

When Jezebel heard this news she threatened to kill Elijah so he fled to Beersheba and then on to Mount Horeb. Here God spoke to him in 'a still small voice', telling him to return to Israel and anoint Jehu as its king and Elisha as the new prophet who would follow in his place. When Elijah died, he was taken up to Heaven in a fiery chariot

Like other major prophets, Elijah was fearless in his fight against evil and preached the message of faith in God in spite of all opposition. He has been the subject of more legends than any other Bible hero. He is depicted as partly human, partly divine. His main purpose was to counsel and protect the common folk in times of trouble—a kind of invisible household friend. He is alleged to have been tolerant of human failings, pleading their cause before God, and giving material help to the poor.

The folklore image of Elijah is often that of a simple Jew, shabbily dressed, with a pack on his back, trudging along footsore and weary. He appears to those in distress, always ready to help them in their hour of need. It is only after Elijah has departed that his true identity is discovered.

Many of the legends told about Elijah are based on the belief that he did not die like other mortals but was 'translated' to Heaven while still alive, swept up by a whirlwind in a chariot of fire.

Elijah has also been associated with the coming of the Messiah, since the time when the Prophet Malachi foretold that God would send Elijah as His messenger. In addition folk concepts suggest that God assigned Elijah the unique role of guide and helper to the souls of men who are welcomed in the World-to-Come.

In orthodox Jewish homes it is the custom during the *Seder* service held on the eve of the Passover festival to pour a cup of wine ready for Elijah. At the appointed time during the reading of the *Haggada* the youngest child present is sent to open the door in order 'to let Elijah in'. This symbolic gesture invites the Prophet as an honoured guest at the festival which celebrates the freeing of the children of Israel from slavery in Egypt.

The prophet's pupil

The rabbis of old upheld the strong Jewish tradition of piety, wisdom and learning. They had a great following of devoted disciples who vied with each other as to whom among their learned teachers had the finest reputation. Rabbi Joshua ben Levi was among these eminent rabbis, famous not only in Jerusalem but in every farflung corner of the land.

More than anything else Rabbi Joshua wanted to meet the Prophet Elijah and to this end he prayed and fasted and repeatedly asked the Almighty God to grant his dearest wish.

One evening, not long after the last 'amen' had been sung at the end of the evening service in the synagogue, Rabbi Joshua, his prayer shawl tucked under his arm was walking home, when the Prophet Elijah appeared:
'Your fervent prayers to God have been answered,' said Elijah. 'Why did you ask to see me?'

At first Rabbi Joshua was only too delighted and excited just to feast his eyes on the great prophet. But then he collected himself and answered modestly: 'I would rather be a pupil than a teacher. I am sure that I would be a much better rabbi and my teaching would have more depth if I could learn wisdom from you.' He gazed at the Prophet with deep longing and then added: 'After all,' he said, 'you, more than anyone else next to God, can give me the best possible education.'

Elijah hesitated then replied: 'Very well I will take you with me on one condition—under no circumstances must you question my actions! You may learn from observation only and if you break your silence I will leave you.'

Rabbi Joshua promised faithfully to obey and the two set off at a brisk pace.

It was late and very dark by the time they reached the edge of the city. Elijah stopped outside a poor tumbledown shack and knocked at the door. It was answered by a frail old man who welcomed the travellers in.
'Come in, come in, you must be cold and tired,' he said. 'As you can see we do not have much to offer, but at least my wife and I can provide you with a little something to eat and a place to sleep.'

And in spite of their protests, the old man shared a loaf of bread with his guests and insisted on them using their beds, while the old man and his wife slept on the floor on a pile of straw.

When Rabbi Joshua woke in the morning, the prophet and the old couple were already up and about. Elijah was trying to console them for the sudden death of their goat. The rabbi knew at once that this was the prophet's doing and when they were out of earshot he protested: 'You must have asked God to strike down the goat, but why? These poor kind people have shown us the most genuine hospitality, and yet you repay them by killing their one and only meagre source of livelihood?'

Elijah looked sternly at the rabbi and put his finger to his lips—to remind him of his promise.

The rabbi was forced into silence and did his best to control his indignation and the torrent of questions he wanted to ask.

They left the poor couple's hovel and walked all day until they reached a well-to-do neighbourhood to call at the house of a wealthy merchant. By that time they were tired and the smell of cooking coming from the kitchen made them weak with hunger. But, in sharp contrast to the previous night, Elijah and his pupil were neither invited into the spacious house, nor were they offered anything to drink or a morsel of food to eat. Instead they were shown—grudgingly—to the stable where they spent a cold disturbed night with only the restless horses stamping in their stalls for company.

Rabbi Joshua was starving when he awoke the next morning and the sight that met his eyes did not improve his temper. The previous evening they had noticed the wooden gate to the rich man's house lying on its side on the ground. It had clearly been damaged, for it was wrenched off its hinges and was awaiting repair. He just caught sight of Elijah's lips moving silently when, in the next moment, a handsome new gate replaced the old one. Joshua bit his lips in anger.
'Why on earth should the prophet save this

tight-fisted merchant from the expense of replacing his own gate?' he thought. 'How dare he help him when he refused us even the most basic hospitality?'

And seething with injustice, Rabbi Joshua broke his pledge and confronted the prophet: 'Perhaps, after all, I am not the model pupil I thought I was,' Rabbi Joshua said wryly, 'but I can no longer hold my peace when I see how you have made life harder for the poor couple who were so kind to us, and have helped a wealthy man who treated us badly.'

The prophet answered: 'I can see you will not rest until I explain my actions, so listen carefully. I asked you to observe, but I know that you cannot see in the same way as I do. You could not have known that the Angel of Death was in the poor man's house when we arrived. He had come for the wife and I pleaded with God to take the goat instead. That good couple will have many years together now and somehow they will manage to replace the goat. As for the rich man who treated us so shabbily, I replaced his gate for one reason only. Being of a mean temperament he would have undertaken the work himself rather than go to the expense of hired labour. I knew that just inside the gate a bag of gold coins had been buried years before, which he would have unearthed. Replacing the gate was the only way of preventing him from finding it.'

Then Elijah embraced Rabbi Joseph and spoke gently to him: 'A diligent pupil like yourself should learn one important lesson. If you see a heartless and selfish man who seems to prosper and a kind-hearted man who seems to be full of sorrow and distress, do not be deceived. God is righteous and his judgement goes beyond man's understanding. He moves in mysterious ways and no one should question Him.'

And the Prophet Elijah gave Rabbi Joshua his blessing and disappeared.

Jonah and the whale

The story of Jonah is set in the period of the great Assyrian Empire in the eighth century before the Common Era. Assyria was then the major power in the Near East with the city of Nineveh as its capital. The Bible states that Nineveh had a population of one hundred and twenty thousand people. Jonah, whose name in Hebrew means a dove, came from a little town near Nazareth in the Land of Israel. He is the fifth of the twelve minor, or less important, prophets and the hero of the book in the Hebrew Bible which bears his name. Unlike the other books of the prophets, the Book of Jonah tells a short story. Its most important message is a moral one, and it illustrates God's mercy and compassion for all those who repent and seek forgiveness for their sins. The story of Jonah is read in synagogues during the afternoon service of the Day of Atonement—the most solemn day in the Hebrew calendar when Jews all over the world pray to God to forgive their sins.

It was no longer a secret that the people of Nineveh were incapable of distinguishing between right and wrong. They had lost their faith in God, turned their backs on decency and preferred all that was evil. They behaved in such a decadent and sinful way that God felt it was time to intervene.

He spoke to Jonah: 'Wherever I look I see the terrible wickedness of the people of Nineveh. Go there at once and preach; warn them that I will punish them. They have forty days in which to repent, otherwise their city

will be destroyed and everyone in it will perish.'

The trouble with Jonah was that although on the one hand he was a God-fearing and righteous man, he also had a stubborn streak. 'I know exactly what will happen,' he argued to himself, 'in the first place God may threaten the inhabitants of Nineveh with destruction, but He is too compassionate to carry it out. As soon as I caution them, they will repent and the Almighty will forgive them, whereas I believe that those who sin deserve to be punished. As far as I can see it will be a wasted journey.'

Having satisfied himself that his reasoning was sound and that there would be no real virtue in going to Nineveh, Jonah decided to avoid the issue, disobey God and escape. But how was he to get away? Jonah was so intent on shelving his responsibilities that he made no firm plans. However, everything seemed to fall into place. He made for the seaport of Jaffa, and as soon as he arrived there he began making inquiries about a passage on any boat ready to sail.

As luck would have it he found a ship bound for Tarshish in Spain. Jonah agreed his fare with the captain, went aboard, and with a fair wind blowing, they were soon underway. Tired out from the strain of the last few days, Jonah went below to sleep.

He might have been comforted with the saying, 'Out of sight, out of mind,' but he had not reckoned with the powers of all-seeing God. The ship was making good headway when there was an ominous change in the weather. The atmosphere became close and sticky, and the bright blue skies were darkened by menacing black clouds. With a deafening crash, the sky glowed with flashes of lightning and seconds later the boat was engulfed in the grip of a roaring hurricane. The winds howled, the waves were whipped up into a fury and passengers and crew clung to each other in terror, trying to shield themselves from the force of the driving gusts of rain.

The captain, fearing his ship would split up under the strain of the storm, implored everyone to pray to their gods.
'Someone aboard my ship has brought a bad omen,' he shouted above the noise of the storm.

'The gods must be very angry to send a storm like this. Whoever it is had better pray hard, make vows and promise to offer sacrifices. If the gods are not appeased soon we shall all be drowned.' And when there was still no sign of the storm abating he ordered the crew to offload heavy pieces of cargo into the sea in an attempt to keep the ship afloat.

While the captain was down in the hold supervising the work he found Jonah asleep on a pile of sail cloths. The captain was most surprised that he had not been disturbed by the tossing of the ship. He shook Jonah: 'How can you possibly sleep through such a terrible storm?' he asked. 'Get up and call on your god for help before it is too late.'

As soon as Jonah went up on deck into the gale, and saw the passengers weeping and praying, his heart sank for he knew only too well what had happened. And when the superstitious sailors cast lots to find out who was to blame for the bad luck, Jonah had a premonition that it would fall on him.

And it happened just as Jonah had feared. The sailors were upset and frightened, and yet curious. They plied him with questions: 'Who are you, and where have you come from? What terrible sin have you committed to bring such a calamity upon us?'

And Jonah's reply came straight from the heart. 'I am a Hebrew from the Land of Israel, I do not pray to idols or your gods, but to the One God, the God of the universe. I have disobeyed Him by trying to hide from my duties and this tempest has been sent as God's retribution.' And Jonah was resolute. Turning to the captain he said, 'But none of you have any part in my quarrel with God and I have no wish to endanger your lives. Throw me into the sea to appease the Almighty and to calm the storm.'

The captain and the sailors talked among themselves. They were reluctant to see a man drown despite his convincing explanation. They tried again to row the boat to shore but the situation was hopeless. Then, as a last resort, they prayed to Jonah's God: 'O, Lord, save us all from drowning, and do not charge us with the death of an innocent man.'

With that they lowered Jonah over the side and in an instant the sea was stilled and the hurricane died away. And everyone on board worshipped God in gratitude.

Meanwhile the waters closed above Jonah's head and he sank down, down into the depths of the deep ocean. Just when he thought that his end had come he dropped into a yawning black cavity—the mouth of a giant whale! And there he stayed, in that cavernous place, in the pitch darkness. for three long days and three even longer nights.

During that dreadful time Jonah was aware of God's great presence. He did not need to be told that he was there on trial, with time to think and reflect. And the more he thought the more he felt wretched and humbled. 'Almighty God, do not forsake me in my hour of need,' he prayed. 'I defied You and tried to evade my duties. I will take an oath and pledge my word of honour that I will faithfully carry out Your commands. I beseech You to send me a sign.'

And Jonah was given a second chance. God ordered the whale to spew him out on to dry land. Then He gave Jonah this command: 'Go to Nineveh and denounce the citizens as I have told you.'

This time there were no arguments, no attempts to escape, no delaying tactics. Jonah set off with God to guide him. When he arrived in Nineveh, he saw for himself that God's description of its inhabitants was only too true. The people were violent and cruel and they had lost all their religious faith.

Jonah carried out God's instructions to the letter. He preached to the king and to the people and he made them see clearly the effects of their evil and selfish ways. He told them that unless they reformed, within forty days the city and all its inhabitants would be destroyed.

The effects of Jonah's proclamation were immediate. The entire population from the king down to the most humble citizen went into deep mourning. They fasted, dressed themselves in sackcloth and put ashes on their heads to symbolize their sorrow.

With each passing day the people returned to God's holy law. They repented honestly and sincerely and called on God to forget their sinful past. And God was satisfied that they had renewed their covenant with Him and were genuine penitents; and He forgave them.

Everyone in the city was filled with joy and gratitude—everyone except Jonah. He was angry.
'O God, I knew You would not punish these people and that is why I tried before to escape to Tarshish. I know You are merciful and bear no grudge, but why then did You bring me here?' And Jonah walked away from the city, on and on until he was exhausted and wanted nothing more than to lie down and die.

Then God spoke again to Jonah: 'Do you think you have a right to be so angry?' But Jonah refused to answer. He remained silent and brooding.

During the night God caused a gourd tree to spring up so that the following day its leafy branches would protect Jonah from the burning sun. And Jonah was more than grateful for the cool shade it provided. The next morning, however, God blighted the tree until it shrivelled away, and then He sent a scorching east wind. Jonah sat on, covered in stinging dust from the desert wind, with the pitiless sun beating down on his head, until he could bear it no longer. He begged God to take his life.

God spoke again to Jonah: 'Are you still angry?'

Jonah explained that he was resentful because He had taken away the gourd tree. 'It was such a beautiful tree. I hated to watch it wither and die away,' he said.

And God replied: 'Why should you feel sorry for that tree which grew in one night and withered in the next? You had no part in its planting, or watering, nor did you watch it grow from a young sapling. But I have given my love and care and attention to the people of Nineveh. Should I not feel for them and spare their lives now they have repented and have learned, at last, to distinguish right from wrong?'

And Jonah bowed his head in deep remorse. He had learned that only honest and true repentance would appease God's anger and atone for wrongdoing and sin.

Tales from the Talmud

The Talmud is the name of a body of Jewish religious writings, second only in importance to the Torah and the other Books of the Hebrew Bible.

The Torah consists of the five books of Moses—Genesis, Exodus, Leviticus, Numbers and Deuteronomy—which are known by the collective title of The Law. These laws were written down, according to tradition, by Moses.

The Talmud consists of two sections: the Mishnah and the Gemara. The Mishnah is a collection of laws based on the Bible and the Gemara consists of lengthy commentaries on the Mishnah. In total the Talmud comprises twelve volumes. The contents of both the Mishnah and the Gemara were originally oral, handed on by spoken teaching. They were only written down much later, in the early centuries of the Common Era. Thus the Torah is known as the Written Law and, the Talmud, namely the Mishnah and Gemara are together known as the Oral Law.

There are two versions of the Talmud. The Babylonian Talmud was completed in Babylon, where there was a large and ancient Jewish community, about the end of the fifth century of the Common Era. The Jerusalem Talmud, or the Talmud of the West, received its final form in Palestine about the end of the third century of the Common Era. The Babylonian version is longer and it is considered to be the more comprehensive of the two.

The Jews did not separate laws and customs from religion, so the Talmud contains much that at first glance appears to have nothing to do with religion at all. In fact it deals with every aspect of Jewish life and behaviour and includes, among other things, medical cures, commercial advice, stories about individuals, scientific, philosophical and historical matters, as well as an explanation and expansion of the Mishnah.

To this day many orthodox Jews spend their entire lives in the study of the Torah and the Talmud. The Torah contains a mass of laws and commandments, not all of them easily understandable. They require a deep and specialized knowledge, an understanding of the commentaries, and a mastery of the explanations which they contain. Torah study provides the means for learning the principles and details necessary to carry out the commandments properly.

The root of the Hebrew word Torah is 'teaching'. It teaches man the path he should follow, and is indeed a guide to fulfilling the commandments. Over the centuries Judaism has developed a profound respect for the study of the Torah, a respect which is summed up in this quotation from the Talmud: 'These are the things, the fruits of which a man enjoys in this world, while the reward remains for him in the World-to-Come: honouring one's father and mother, performing deeds of kindness, making peace between man and his fellow man. But the study of the Torah is equal to them all.'

This chapter contains stories drawn from the extraordinary range of characters and episodes mentioned in the Talmud. They represent only a tiny fraction of the abundance of material which it contains. And since the whole of the Torah and the Talmud are concerned above all with teaching the right way to live, all of them emphasize the moral and religious obligations which a pious man must undertake in order to lead the kind of life of which God would approve.

King Alexander's questions

In the year 333 B C E King Alexander of Macedonia and his army made a triumphant entry into the city of Jerusalem. A group of wise Jews came out to greet the conqueror.
'I have some questions to ask you,' he told them, 'and if you are able to answer them all, and give me proof of your wisdom, I will allow you to go in peace.'

The wise men bowed low and sat down to listen to the king.
'Which is the greater distance,' he asked, 'that between heaven and earth or that between east and west?'
'That between east and west, Your Majesty. The sun rises in the east, when it is so distant that it can be observed without the eyes being dazzled by the sun's rays. The same thing occurs when it sets in the west. But when the sun is high overhead in the centre of heaven its great light is so blinding that it is impossible to look at it with the naked eye. At that point the sun in heaven is nearer to earth than either east or west. It follows, therefore, that heaven is nearer to earth than east is to west.'

King Alexander nodded and asked a second question: 'Which was created first—light or darkness?'

When they heard this, the wise men hesitated, then the leader whispered to the others, 'If we say that darkness is mentioned first in the Scriptures, the king will, no doubt, become more curious. He will want to know what there is above the heavens and beneath the earth, and what existed before heaven and earth were created, and what will exist after they have ceased to be. We had better tell him that the question is too difficult.' The others agreed and their leader spoke to the king:
'Sire, there is no man on earth who could satisfactorily explain the complex nature of your question.'

The king seemed satisfied. 'Very well,' he continued, ' I will ask more straightforward questions—for example, who is wise?'
'The person who can see the consequence of his actions.'
'Who is a hero?'
'The man who can control his passions.'
'Who is rich?'
'The one who is contented with his lot.'
'When does a man preserve his life?'
'When he kills himself—in the sense of restraining all his desire.'
'When does a man bring about his own death?'
'When he clings to life—in the sense of allowing his desires to overcome him.'
'How should a man behave in order to gain the friendship of others?'
'He should shun glory, and despise kingship and with it dominion over others.'
'That is not a sensible answer,' Alexander retorted. 'It seems to me that the opposite is true. A person who wishes to win friends must strive for glory. Then he will be in a position to help those who need it.'

The wise men remained silent, and Alexander asked another question. 'Is it better to live on dry land or on the water?'

'Dry land is better for man, as anyone who has been to sea will tell you. Sailors never seem to find peace of mind when they are afloat, but live in constant anxiety.'

Having come to the end of his list of questions, the king then asked the wise men, 'Which one among you is the wisest?'

'We are all equally wise, Your Majesty.'

'Why then do you keep yourselves to yourselves and disobey my laws? Have you no fear of me, the great Alexander of Macedonia, conqueror of the world?'

'O King, day in and day out the forces of evil come to tempt us. Glory to him who disobeys!'

The king was furious when he heard their reply.

'Do you realize that at a mere signal to my officers, I can have you all put to death?' he raged.

'We are well aware that this is the case,' the wise men replied calmly. 'Nevertheless we do not think that it is becoming for the great King Alexander to lie to his subjects. With respect, Your Majesty, you promised to let us go in peace after we had answered all your questions.'

The king saw that they were right and smoothed his ruffled pride. Then he called his stewards and instructed them to present the wise men with costly gifts from his treasury. When the ceremony was over, he stood up to leave.

'Thank you all,' he said 'and now I will bid you farewell and set sail for Africa.'

'For Africa!' the wise men repeated in astonishment. 'Sire, are you not aware that between here and Africa are mountain peaks that almost touch the sky? They will be a dark and formidable barrier, and make your journey a difficult one.'

'Can you advise me then?' asked Alexander.

'You will need a team of asses from distant Arabia,' the wise men informed him. 'They are sure-footed and can see in the dark. Make strong reins of flax for the animals and hold on to them firmly. In this way you will be able to pass safely through the mountains.'

And the king followed the advice of the wise men in every detail and reached his destination in safety.

Honi the rainmaker

Folktales throughout the world include many themes connected with rain. Some peoples believed in the existence of a rain god, or a water god, or a saint whose special responsibility was water. Since time immemorial, whenever there is a severe drought and the crops have shrivelled and died from lack of water, men have prayed to their own special god to bless their harvest with nourishing rain.

In the Jewish religion, however, prayers are always addressed to the One God who rules the universe. At the time when the Talmud was being compiled it was customary for pious men to pray to God, asking Him to send abundant rain for the parched fields. There was a widespread belief that God always listened to the prayers of the righteous, particularly those who had experienced some bitter suffering.

During the reign of Yannai, one of the last of the Hasmonean kings of Israel, in the year 103 BCE, there was a severe drought in the land of Israel. The farmers were in despair. The soil was hard and cracked, the grapes had shrivelled on the vines, and the grain harvests had failed. 'If we do not have rain very soon, the wells will dry up, our animals will die, and so will we,' one of the farmers muttered to his father.

'Let us go and speak to Honi, the sage, and ask him to pray for rain. They say that God has never refused him any request,' the old man suggested.

They set off to find Honi the sage and when their friends and neighbours heard of the plan, they followed, so that soon a large crowd had gathered, all with one aim—to implore Honi to appeal to the Almighty on their behalf.

Honi was a man of immense spiritual power. He spent his days in the study of the Torah, interpreting the true meaning of God's Holy Law and he was famous throughout the Holy Land for his piety and learning. His heart was filled with compassion at the sight of the group of worried, haggard-looking men and women walking slowly towards him.

'What can I do to help you, good people?' he asked.

The farmer who led the group answered. 'The heavens are closed against us, we have had no rain for weeks together, and there are no crops to harvest. If the drought continues, we will all starve to death. We have come to ask you to save us—please, pray to God and ask Him to send rain.'

Every eye was fixed on Honi's face as his lips moved in a silent prayer to God. When he had finished they all looked up at the skies, watching and waiting for a sign. But nothing happened and nothing changed.

When Honi realized that his prayer had had no effect he gently pushed back the crowd, took a stick and drew the outline of a large circle in the dust. Then he walked into the centre of it, raised his arms and this time prayed out loud in a voice full of emotion: 'Lord of the Universe, I swear by Your Holy Name that I will not move from here until You have taken pity on Your children and sent us rain.'

Once more all eyes strained upwards to the heavens, watching and waiting. Then a light shower of rain began to fall drop by drop. But Honi was not satisfied.
'Gracious Lord, I did not pray for little droplets, but for sufficient rain to fill all the cisterns and raise the level of the water in the wells.' And the silent crowd hardly dared to breathe as they lined the edge of the circle, watching Honi standing alone in its centre.

Suddenly they heard a distant rumble of thunder coming nearer and nearer. Dark black clouds rolled overhead covering the scorching rays of the sun. Then the rain began to fall in torrents. Moments later Honi and the crowd of farmers were drenched to the skin, the line of the circle was completely washed away and the dust beneath their feet was turned to mud. But no one moved.

For the third time Honi spoke to God: 'Almighty God, I beseech you—send rain of goodwill, blessing and graciousness.' And this time the rain fell gently but steadily, just the right amount to nourish and revive the parched land. The hearts of the people overflowed with gratitude and they went to the Temple to give thanks to God. From that time Honi became known as Honi the Circle.

When the excitement had died down and he was able to return to his studies, Honi opened his book of psalms. He was curious about one particular sentence which had perplexed him for a long time. He read: 'When God had brought us out of exile back to the Holy Land we were like dreamers.'

He tried to imagine how his ancestors had felt when the Temple was destroyed by their enemies. They had been forced to live in exile in a strange land for seventy long and lonely years. Could that time have passed by like a dream? Did the Children of Israel feel like strangers when they returned once again to the land of Israel?

One day, still pondering on the verse, he decided to leave his studies for a while. He sat astride his donkey and rode through the countryside. It felt good to be outside: the fields were green, the crops were flourishing and the air was heavy with fragrance.

He rode along until he came across a farmer planting a tree. 'Shalom aleichem, peace be with you,' he called out to the farmer. 'What is the name of the tree you are planting?'
'It is a carob tree,' the farmer replied.
'How long will it take to mature and bear fruit?' Honi asked.
'About seventy years or so.'

Honi stood, deep in thought, watching the farmer at work. 'Since you will not be alive to enjoy its fruit, why do you take such time and trouble to plant it?'

The farmer straightened his back, and leaned on his spade. 'The reason is simple enough. I am following a long tradition. At this time of the year I can enjoy the fruit of the trees which my father and grandfather planted when they were alive. This one,' and the farmer pointed to the young sapling, 'will, I hope, bear fruit for my grandchildren.'

Honi nodded to the old farmer and rode on. After a while he began to feel hungry and tired so he looked for a suitable place to rest. He noticed a cave nearby, tethered his donkey outside, and was thankful to find that it was dark and cool inside—just the place to escape the heat of the sun. Before he had had a chance to eat the food he had brought with him, his whole body became heavy with an overwhelming tiredness, his eyelids drooped, and try as he might he could not fight off the waves of sleep which engulfed him.

Honi slept on and on, and days, weeks, months and then years passed. The tangle of shrubs and climbing plants around the mouth of the cave continued to put out new shoots and tendrils which spread right across the entrance. A traveller riding past would never have suspected what lay hidden from view behind the lush undergrowth.

Time went by and the widespread searches to find Honi the Circle were abandoned, and speculation about his strange disappearance came to an end. The years passed. His wife died, his son married and was blessed with a son of his own. Honi was forgotten by everyone except the rabbis who read his scholarly works.

Then one day the dense foliage which sealed the entrance to the cave dried out, shrivelled and fell away. A shaft of warm sunshine woke Honi from his long sleep. He stood up, stretched and walked out of the cave to untie his donkey. But when he found, in its place, a pile of dry bones, he could not understand what had happened. He noticed too, that the landscape was unfamiliar. He seemed to be standing deep in a forest, where once there had been open fields.

Honi walked on, trying to make sense of his surroundings and soon came upon a man picking fruit from the lower branches of a tall tree. Honi greeted the farmer. 'Peace be with you,' he called out as he approached. He noticed that the farmer's basket was full of locust-beans, the fruit of the carob tree. 'I see you are gathering the fruits of your labour,' he remarked in a friendly way.

The farmer looked up at Honi in some surprise. 'You are obviously ignorant of the laws of nature or you would not have made such a remark,' he said. 'It takes seventy years for the carob tree to bear fruit. My late grandfather planted this tree. Unfortunately, he did not live long enough to reap the harvest, but, as you can see, he did not work in vain.'

An icy chill clutched at Honi's heart when he heard the farmer's words. 'Dear God, could I possibly have slept for seventy years?' he said under his breath. 'What will become of me now?' Then he pulled himself together. 'I must find out if any of my family and friends still survive.'

When he reached his home town he tried to get his bearings. But everything had changed and he no longer recognized familiar landmarks. He felt lost and helpless and in desperation stopped passers-by to ask if they knew where his son lived.

When he had all but given up hope an old woman was able to help.

'Honi's son is dead and his grandson has inherited the property,' she said. 'You had better go and see him.' And she gave him the necessary directions.

Soon Honi was standing outside a building which he dimly remembered was the family home. A tall man opened the door and asked Honi his business.
'I am Honi the Circle, your grandfather,' Honi told him. 'I have been asleep in a cave for seventy years, but thank God the spell has been broken and I have returned home.'

The man was immediately on his guard. 'Look here, old man, if you want some food, just say so. There is no need to invent wild stories. Wait here, and I will bring you some bread.'

As soon as the man disappeared inside the house, Honi brushed away his tears and turned away. 'Even my own grandson does not know me,' he muttered to himself bitterly.

He wandered around not knowing where to go or what to say until he came to a synagogue. There he met a group of rabbis who invited him to join them in the study of the Torah. It was not long before he surpassed them all in Talmudic knowledge. The oldest rabbi congratulated Honi on his great learning: 'You are as wise as the famous Honi the Circle was in his day.'

Honi answered joyfully, 'But I am Honi, don't you recognize me?'

The rabbis were annoyed. 'You should have been satisfied with our compliments, instead of asking to be honoured like a saint,' they said.

With a heavy heart Honi realized that even the learned rabbis did not understand. He left the synagogue and wandered round the streets, asking after old friends and relatives, all of whom were long since dead. There was no one who cared, not one familiar face to greet him and offer him hospitality at their table. He was utterly alone, like a stranger from a distant land. 'Now I understand only too well the meaning of the psalm and what it feels like to be a stranger in a foreign land. No wonder then that we were like dreamers when God brought us out of exile. But what use is my knowledge to me now?' he asked himself. 'The man who planted the carob tree for his grandson was much more fortunate than I. He, at least, is remembered with love and affection. As for me, neither my grandson nor the rabbis recognize me. Dear Lord have I not lived long enough?'

And God had mercy on his soul. Leaving the town behind him, Honi walked away, on and on, never stopping until he reached the cave where he had rested so long. There he lay down and slept, and died peacefully in his sleep.

The romance of Akiba

Kalba Sabua, who lived in Jerusalem, was a very rich man. He had an only daughter, Rachel, who was as beautiful as she was clever. Kalba's house became the focal point of a steady procession of eligible bachelors from the most influential families in the land, who came to court Rachel. But one after the other, kindly but firmly, she turned down their offers of marriage.

Kalba was beginning to lose patience with his fastidious daughter. 'Surely you can find a suitable partner from among all your suitors?' he snapped.
'My dear father, you know full well that neither wealth nor good family connections will influence my choice,' Rachel told him. 'The man I marry must have a fine character and a generous heart.'

It happened about this time that the head herdsman of Kalba's large herds of goats and flocks of sheep hired a new shepherd called Akiba. Rachel saw him from time to time driving the flocks to fresh pastures or bringing them back to the fold in the evening. At first they merely exchanged a friendly greeting, but gradually a mutual understanding flourished between them. There was an inner warmth and strength of character about the young man which attracted Rachel, and it was not long before the young couple were in love.

Rachel knew that her father would not take kindly to her choice, and she needed all her courage to stand up to his strong objections. 'Have you gone mad?' Kalba ranted when he heard the news. 'You could be betrothed to any one of the finest young men in the land and you ask me to agree to your marrying a mere shepherd? Surely you cannot be serious.'
'I love Akiba and I want to marry him,' Rachel said quietly, 'and nothing you say can change my mind.'

But Kalba raved on. 'I cannot believe that you can behave in such a foolish way. My servant for a son-in-law? Impossible!'

Rachel remained silent, and Kalba knew it was useless to argue. 'Very well, if you insist on marrying this man I swear a solemn oath that I will disinherit you.'

Rachel loved her father dearly and was saddened to see him so embittered. But she was convinced that she had made the right decision. Soon after, the young people were married and Rachel left her father's house for ever.

In spite of the stark contrast between the luxury of her own home and their new dwelling place, Rachel was very happy. The young couple lived in a tent near Jerusalem and slept on a simple pallet filled with straw, which tended to scatter whenever a strong wind blew. They had very little money and often had nothing to eat except dry bread.

Akiba grew sad and thoughtful. 'Perhaps I was too selfish in asking you to live with me in poverty, when I know the kind of life you might have had if you were married to a rich man,' he sighed.
'My dear Akiba, can't you see that I am happy? A life of splendour would be meaningless and empty if I could not share it with you,' Rachel answered.

Just then they heard a plaintive voice outside their tent.
'Who is there and what do you want?' Rachel asked.
'For God's sake have pity on me. My wife is sick and I need some straw for her to lie on. Can you spare some?'

Rachel gave some of their straw to the stranger and, when he had thanked her and left, she turned to Akiba. 'As for poverty—you can see for yourself that there are people far worse off than we are.'

Akiba embraced his wife. 'I am, indeed, a fortunate man and God will bless you for these words of comfort.'

Time passed and although Akiba worked hard as a shepherd, he cherished the hope that one day he would be able to study at the Yeshiva—the Jewish Academy—in Jerusalem. At first it seemed simply an impossible dream. Students at the Yeshiva spent long years studying the ancient Hebrew writings and debating the meaning of the Torah—and Akiba could neither read nor write. One evening he told Rachel of his hopes and dreams.

Rachel was overjoyed. 'Nothing would give me greater pleasure than to help you achieve your goal. You must do whatever is necessary. I will not stand in your way.'

Akiba was deeply touched by his wife's unselfishness. When everything was ready for his journey, Rachel accompanied him part of the way. 'I know your new life will not be an easy one, but I will think of you and pray for you. God bless you, Akiba.' And she kissed her husband and turned back.

Akiba walked along the road deep in thought. He was full of apprehensions and doubts. Had he acted responsibly in leaving his wife to fend for herself? Would he be considered too old to study God's Holy Law, and would he live long enough to finish his studies?

He had not gone very far when he saw a group of shepherds sitting down near a spring. While he was chatting to them he noticed that one of the stones at the mouth of the stream was marked with many grooves. 'I wonder how they were formed?' he asked pointing to the grooves.

One of the shepherds replied: 'Year in and year out a steady trickle of water has dropped on to the stone.'

Akiba was greatly encouraged by this. 'If a stone can be shaped in this way, perhaps constant devotion to learning will shape my mind!'

He continued on his journey until he came to a school for children. 'There is no better place to learn to read and write,' he thought, and putting aside any embarrassment he might have felt, he sat down next to the little pupils who welcomed him happily. And there he remained, studying alongside the children, until he felt confident enough to undertake the rigorous studies of the Yeshiva, under the guidance of several eminent rabbis.

Every morning before he went to the Yeshiva, Akiba went to the forest to chop some wood which he sold to earn enough money to buy just enough food to enable him to live. He kept some of the wood for his own use, and the rest he used as a pillow.

Akiba could not afford to leave his studies and visit his wife, but he sent letters and messages to her. Rachel was saddened when she heard about his frugal way of life. Poor as she was, she was determined to help and, as she had no gifts to send, she cut short her beautiful long hair, sold it, and sent the money she received to her husband.

Akiba was a dedicated pupil. He studied day and night and before long he had outstripped all the other students in wisdom and knowledge. If there was a particularly difficult problem concerning rabbinical law to be discussed, or a complicated passage from the Torah to be explained, the students went straight to him for help and advice.

For twelve long years Akiba studied at the Yeshiva. Then, one day he decided that he must go to see Rachel. When he arrived he was about to open the door to the little hut where she lived when he overheard a woman's voice inside.

'You know, Rachel, you have no one to blame but yourself. Your husband has been in Jerusalem for twelve years while you have been living alone in poverty. What on earth will happen to you if he doesn't come back? Your situation would have been very different if you had obeyed your father: you would now be living in the lap of luxury.'

Then Akiba heard Rachel reply, 'If Akiba were here at this very moment, he would listen to my advice. I would not hesitate to tell him to go back to the Yeshiva for another twelve years so that he could continue his studies, undisturbed.'

When he heard this, Akiba knew that, hard as the enforced separation was for both of them, Rachel was right. He suppressed his longing to be with her and returned to the Yeshiva.

And so Akiba continued to study and teach, spending time at different Jewish academies throughout the land of Israel. By this time his fame had spread so widely that he had a following of thousands of devoted students who revered him for his knowledge and piety. In this way twelve more years passed. After this time, Akiba felt the need to continue his work once more in the Yeshiva in Jerusalem. As soon as the inhabitants heard the good news, they lined the streets to welcome him back. Rachel was

among the excited onlookers in the crowd. One of her neighbours commented on her shabby dress.

'Rachel you cannot be seen in that! I will be happy to lend you something more festive. After all, welcoming the famous Rabbi Akiba is a special occasion for us all.'

'I know he will be more concerned with what people are, rather than with what they wear,' replied Rachel quietly. And the matter was closed.

Just then Akiba appeared, surrounded by hundreds of students. Rachel managed to elbow her way to the front of the jostling crowd and knelt down at Akiba's feet. She was overcome with deep emotion as she kissed the hem of his robe. Some of his followers were on the point of pushing her to one side, when Akiba prevented them.

'Stop that at once,' he ordered, helping Rachel to her feet. 'This is my wife Rachel. If it were not for her unstinting devotion and support, I would not now be your teacher. I have her alone to thank for encouraging me to devote myself to a life of study and learning.' And he took Rachel's worn hand in his. 'My loyal wife has waited for me, without complaint, for twenty-four long years.'

Unknown to either Akiba or Rachel, Kalba Sabua was one of those who had come not only to welcome Rabbi Akiba, but also to ask his advice on a certain matter which was troubling him. He waited patiently until he was invited into the rabbi's lodgings. Without making his identity known, Akiba asked him in what way he could help.

'Many years ago my daughter married, against my wishes, a poor shepherd boy. I was so angry at the time that I took a solemn oath to disinherit her.'

'On what grounds did you reject the shepherd?' Akiba asked.

'He was poor and ignorant, and I believed then that my daughter was marrying beneath her.'

'And where are your daughter and her husband now?'

'May God help me when I tell you that I have not seen either of them for twenty-four years,' Kalba sobbed. 'If you will release me from my oath, I will search for them as long as the Almighty God gives me breath in my body.'

Rachel overheard everything from an adjoining room. Unable to restrain her feelings any longer, she burst into the room. 'Father, oh my dear father, I am your daughter Rachel, and this is your son-in-law, Akiba.'

The reunion was filled with joy and happiness, laughter and tears.
'My dear daughter,' said Kalba. 'Forgive me, you were right to have married Akiba and may God bless you both.'

The test of a true friend

Long, long ago there lived a philosopher called Arvas. As he was growing old, he began to look back on his long life. One day he asked his son: 'How many people do you know whom you could count as your friends?'
'A great number,' his son answered proudly.
'I am much older than you, and yet in all my long life I have found only one good friend,' said Arvas. 'Remember that only when he has been tested and tried can a man be called a friend. Don't you think you are being rather rash to boast of so many? Put them to the test and find out for yourself how genuine they really are!'
'How shall I do that?' the son asked.
'Listen carefully,' Arvas said. 'Go to the market, buy an animal carcass and ask the butcher to cut it up in pieces and put it in a sack. Then carry it to one of your friends and tell him: Dear friend, I beg of you to help me! I have just killed a man in self defence! Help me to bury him behind your house, and no one will be any the wiser. You will surely save my life if you agree.'

The son obeyed his father's instructions to the letter. Then he went to one of his friends and pleaded with him to help bury the sack. His friend took one look at the blood-stained bag and shouted: 'You must be mad to expect me to get mixed up in your crime. Get out of here at once and stay away!'

Disappointed by this abrupt response, the son dragged the sack from friend to friend. Each of them refused in a different way but the message was clear. No one wanted to be involved in any way. Hurt and dejected the young man returned to his father and described his experiences.

Arvas nodded wisely. 'It comes as no surprise, on the contrary it is precisely what I had expected. When a man prospers his friends seem to multiply, but they vanish like mist when he gets into difficulties. Take the sack to my good friend and see how he behaves.'

The son agreed and when his father's friend came to the door, he told him who he was, repeated his tale of woe and begged him to bury the sack in secret. Without questioning him further the man sprang into action.
'Be quick! Come into the house before the neighbours see you.' He hid the son and his sack until he had managed to send his wife and children on an errand. As soon as they were alone, they went into the yard and began to dig a grave.

Then the son called a halt to the work and explained the true nature of his visit. 'I came to test you, and you have given me abundant proof of the nature of a good friend!' he said.

When the young man returned home, he told his father how moved he had been by his friend's kindness. 'But tell me, Father, if you regard this man as merely a good friend, is there anyone in the world fortunate enough to have a *true* friend?'
'I have never been blessed with such a treasure,' Arvas replied, 'but I have heard about one.' And he told his son this story of true friendship.

Once there were two young merchants, one of whom lived in Egypt and the other in Babylon. They had never met but kept in touch by sending messages with the travellers who delivered the merchandise which they traded with each other.

On one occasion, however, the Babylonian merchant journeyed to Egypt with a caravan of goods. As soon as the Egyptian merchant heard that his friend was coming he made lavish preparations to welcome him to his home where he was treated as an honoured guest. His servants waited on him hand and foot and nothing was considered too much trouble.

Barely a week after he arrived, the Babylonian merchant fell seriously ill. The most eminent physicians of Egypt were called to examine him and various cures were prescribed. The Egyptian made special arrangements for a young woman to look after him. Each day she carried out the doctors' instructions with skill and patience and gradually she nursed the young man back to health.

When he was fully recovered he thanked his host most sincerely. 'I am more than grateful to the young woman who has devoted so much of her time to me. I really owe my life to her and I would like to make her my wife.'

The Egyptian, who was a single man, did not tell his friend that he was planning to marry the young girl himself. He had sent her, instead of a humble maidservant, to the sick room as a mark of esteem for his invalid friend. But he did not hesitate. 'May God bless you both,' he said. 'I know she will make you a good wife.' And the Egyptian showered the girl with many gifts as well as a handsome dowry.

As soon as he was fit to travel, the merchant prepared for his journey back to Babylon with his bride. Just before they departed, he took off his signet ring and placed it on his host's finger. 'Wear this as a mark of my friendship,' he said.

Years later the prosperous Egyptian merchant got into financial difficulties. In a desperate attempt to economize he sold his big house and sent his servants away. But even these measures were not enough to stave off destitution and in despair he thought of his friend in Babylon. 'If I can survive the difficulties of the journey, I know he will help me,' he thought.

He travelled for many months until, footsore and weary, he arrived in Babylon. He was about to make his way to his friend's house when he looked down at himself in dismay. He was worn out and dirty, his clothes were shabby and dusty and his sandals were definitely the worse for wear.
'What if my friend's servants should think I am a beggar and turn me away?' he said to himself and shuddered at the thought. 'I am too exhausted to go on. I must first find somewhere

to rest and recover my strength.'

As luck would have it, he noticed a wayfarer's shelter on the outskirts of the city. He sat down thankfully and was just about to go to sleep when he was startled by voices raised in anger. He saw two men locked in a violent struggle. One of them pulled out a dagger, stabbed the other several times and ran off leaving the wounded man for dead.

In less than no time a crowd collected and a search began to find the murderer. It did not take the guards very long to drag the Egyptian from the shelter and make him their prime suspect, especially when they discovered that he was a stranger and admitted to having witnessed the crime.

In spite of his strenuous protests that he was innocent, the merchant was thrown into prison. There was no one to turn to for support, there was no one who would listen to him or contact his friend, and the criminal had disappeared. The next morning the judges sentenced him to be hanged.

In those days executions were made into a public spectacle and all the inhabitants of the city came to watch. Among them was the condemned man's friend. The merchant thought he recognized the prisoner in spite of his rags and haggard appearance. And when he noticed the man was wearing the signet ring he had given him, he was certain of his identity. 'Stop! Stop! Free him at once! You cannot hang an innocent man,' he shouted to the judges. 'You have made a terrible mistake—he did not commit the murder—I did!'

The crowd was stunned into an emotional silence while the judges ordered the release of the Egyptian merchant and prepared his friend for the gallows in his place.

Unknown to anyone the murderer stood among the spectators who had gathered around the scaffold. In spite of himself he was deeply stirred by the display of true devotion which he had just witnessed between the two friends. And suddenly he was gripped by a dreadful fear. 'I will surely lose my place in the World to Come, if I allow an innocent man to die for my crime,' he thought.

To the amazement of the onlookers he called out to the judges: 'Release this man immediately! Neither he nor his friend committed this murder. The first man was blamed because he had no one to verify his innocence, and the second shouldered the blame because of the true friendship he felt for the innocent victim. But I am the real murderer—and justice will be done if you hang me.'

And Arvas looked kindly at his son and said, with a note of deep satisfaction in his voice: 'My son, this tale of the merchant from Babylon who was willing to sacrifice his life for the Egyptian—that is the best example I know of true friendship.'

The lost harp

King David's harp made the most beautiful music in the whole world. He kept it always by his side except at night when it hung near the window of his bedroom. In the middle of the night the north wind would blow across its strings, creating a stirring, haunting melody. These wonderful musical sounds woke the king and, as if he were divinely inspired, he began to write. Eloquent words flowed effortlessly from his pen, as he wrote the poems that came to be known as the Psalms of David.

The magic harp had other properties, too. Not only did the wind play on its strings, but it enabled King David to look into the future. There he had a vision of the Temple in Jerusalem which would be built by his son, King Solomon. Sadly he could see tragic events beyond that time when the Temple would be destroyed, and the people of Israel driven into exile to Babylon. He was so tormented and saddened by these dreadful events that he wrote this sad lament:
By the rivers of Babylon,
We sat down and wept,
When we remembered Zion.
There on the willow trees
We hung our harps,
For our captors demanded music and song
and called on us to be merry,
'Sing us one of the songs of Zion' they insisted.
But how could we sing the Lord's song
in a foreign land?

Everything happened exactly as King David had seen in his vision. The walls of the Temple were torn down and the people of Israel were driven into exile. They were poor, oppressed and homeless, always yearning and praying to be able to return to the Holy Land. When that time came at last the Jews began the long task of rebuilding the Temple and Jerusalem.

In those far off days there was an old pious Jew call Shabatai who lived in Jerusalem. He was a musician and skilled craftsman and was well known for making fine lutes and harps. He knew about the wonders of King David's harp and had learned the beautiful psalm by heart.

Whenever he put new strings in one of his own harps, Shabatai wondered what had happened to the magical one. The old man had even heard the legend that King David had used the sinews of a ram to make the harp's strings. According to the legend, it was the very same ram that Abraham had sacrificed to God on Mount Moriah in place of his son, Isaac.

The old man became obsessed with the thought that if only the harp could be found, the Spirit of God would return to bless Jerusalem as it had in the days of King David. This harp had disappeared at the time of the Babylonian exile and Shabatai had no idea where it might be found. Not a day went by without the old man pondering this question. And the more Shabatai thought about it, the more convinced he became that the harp had been hung in the willow trees in Babylon.

Every day whilst he plucked and tuned the strings of his harps, Shabatai thought about the lost one. He even imagined he could see it in a willow tree overhanging the rivers of Babylon. Although no longer young, he made up his mind to find it and return it to Jerusalem. When his friends heard of his plan they thought he had taken leave of his senses. No matter how hard they tried to prevent him from embarking on such a mad venture, Shabatai stood firm. He was overwhelmed with the urge to make this search in spite of all the difficulties and obstacles he might encounter on the way.

Shabatai's wife and family tried to make him see the hopelessness of the plan. How could the harp possibly be found? Where would he even begin to look? The rivers of Babylon flowed for hundreds of miles, their banks thick with willow trees, far too numerous to be counted. Besides, Shabatai was an old man and definitely not strong enough to face the hazards ahead.

Shabatai stubbornly ignored his family's entreaties. Every night he dreamed he glimpsed David's golden harp hanging in the branches of a willow tree, just beyond his reach. The vision was too powerful to resist. One day he closed his workshop, filled a flask with water and a pouch with dates and figs and, leaning heavily on his walking stick, he set off to find the magic harp.

It did not take him long to realize what an immense task he had undertaken. He crossed a dry, arid desert, climbed steep mountains and stumbled downhill to the valleys below. He crossed rivers and streams and went on into another wilderness. On and on he walked, certain that he was being guided by the distant sweet plucking of David's harp, calling to him as it had to King David.

By the time he reached Babylon the effects of the journey were beginning to show. Shabatai looked frail and feeble. Nevertheless he searched along the shores of the rivers and in the branches of the willow trees where the harp might have been hung. It was only when he had searched in vain for several months that he became discouraged. Perhaps, after all, he should have listened to his friends' and family's warnings.

In despair he went to the graves of the pious sages who had died in exile. He lifted up his hands towards heaven and cried: 'Almighty God, listen to the prayer of an old man. I am weak and weary of looking for the magic harp. Send me a sign before I die.' Shabatai prayed long and hard by the tombs, but all he heard was the whispering of the wind.

Suddenly he was startled by a shadow cast from behind. When he turned round he saw a ghostly figure who spoke gently to him: 'What is it that you wish to know?'

Shabatai pleaded to be guided to King David's harp.

The ghostly spirit listened carefully before it replied.
'You have undertaken this long and hard journey for the right reasons,' it said, 'but, alas, you are looking in the wrong place. The psalm says that the harps were hung in the willows of Zion, the Holy Land, not in Babylon. The people simply left them behind because they realized that they could never sing songs of praise to the Lord in a strange land.'

Shabatai listened with rapt attention to these words; it was only after the ghostly shape had vanished that he was convinced it had been none other than the spirit of King David himself. He no longer felt dismayed by such a long and fruitless journey. On the contrary,

Shabatai felt inspired and honoured by King David's appearance. He had learned a valuable secret and still cherished the hope of finding the harp on his return.

The long journey back to Jerusalem was made lighter by the sweet and tender music of David's harp which Shabatai now heard more loudly than before. When, at last, he reached the borders of the land of Israel, it seemed to Shabatai that he could feel a Divine Presence whispering among the trees and flowers. What he had been unable to see for so long now became crystal-clear for the first time. Nothing had really changed. Jerusalem and the Holy Land had never really lost any of their holiness since the time of King David; the Spirit of God was with them still.

There was great rejoicing when Shabatai was reunited with his family once more. Everyone was so pleased to see him safely home again that they quite forgot to ask him about his quest. It was just as well, because Shabatai had decided not to tell anyone of what had happened until he had succeeded in finding the harp.

But the same problems had to be faced. Where was he to begin the search? Shabatai asked himself this question over and over again. One day the answer came to him in a flash of inspiration. He left his long-suffering family once more, but this time for Mount Zion—for although the entire Holy Land is known as Zion there is a mountain which also bears the same name. When he reached the mountain, Shabatai found that he could climb it without difficulty, just as if he were a young man again. And with his new-found youthful energy he looked in every willow tree on the mountain. But there was no harp to be found anywhere. This was more than the old man could bear. He sat down, put his head in his hands, and wept.

Just then the strains of the most beautiful music could be heard in the distance. Shabatai began to walk towards it as if in a trance. When the music grew fainter, he realized he had lost his way, but when it grew louder he knew he was walking in the right direction. In this way Shabatai found himself outside a cave, the entrance of which was hidden behind a willow tree. The cave was filled with a glowing light.

Hypnotized by the sounds—the wonderful music—he walked into the cave. On and on he went, deep into the rock until, at the very far end, he found himself in a bright garden. Shabatai knew at once he was in a sacred place. He gasped in astonishment when he looked around him. From every tree hung a harp, its strings plucked by the wind, creating an orchestra of the most heavenly music. But the most wonderful of all was a golden object, glinting and shimmering from the upper branches of the tallest willow tree. At long last he had found King David's harp. He sat down at the foot of the tree and listened enraptured to that haunting melody—the very strains that had wakened the king and inspired him to write the immortal psalms.

Happy and fulfilled, Shabatai sat on beneath the tree, and some say that he can be found there still, listening as the music of the Spirit of God drifts across the Holy Land, music that is far more beautiful than anyone can imagine.

Brotherly love

Long, long ago in biblical times, there lived two pious, kind-hearted brothers, Menasseh and Simon. Menasseh was married with a wife and family, but Simon was a bachelor and lived by himself. Together they farmed a field which they had inherited from their late father.

There was never a quarrel or a cross word between the two brothers, indeed it was a familiar sight to see them hard at work sharing the ploughing, sowing, harvesting and all the other tasks essential for growing good crops.

As soon as the barley was ripe, one of the brothers cut it with a scythe, while the other bound it into sheaves. It was taken for granted that the results of their joint labours would be divided equally between them. One year the harvest was particularly abundant and yielded two sizeable portions of sheaves which were left side by side in the field ready for threshing into grain. Tired but well-pleased with their hard work, the brothers wished each other goodnight before going home.

Later that night Simon woke up and began to

think things over. 'Menasseh and I have always been happy to share our labours,' he said to himself, 'but I am not so sure we should each take an equal share. After all I am a single man, and I hope that God will bless me with many more years of health and strength. But Menasseh has a wife and a growing family to provide for. His needs are greater than mine.'

The more he thought about it the more he realized how selfish he had been. He decided to put matters right without further delay. He got up and dressed, and with the moon to light his way, he shouldered his pitchfork and strode off to the field. One by one Simon pitched the heavy sheaves of barley from his pile on to Menasseh's. He worked on tirelessly until he had given half his share to his brother. Then, with a feeling of satisfaction, he returned to his house to sleep the sleep of the just.

Unknown to Simon, Menasseh had also been unable to sleep. He confided to his wife. 'I have been thinking about my brother Simon. I do not think it is fair to divide the harvest equally between us. God willing our children will provide for us in our old age, whereas Simon has no one to support him.' Menasseh's wife, Shifra, heartily agreed with her husband and there and then he decided to be as good as his word. He got out of bed, dressed and shouldered his pitchfork. The moon had disappeared behind a cloud by the time Menasseh reached the field, but he worked in the dim light until half of his stack of sheaves had been moved to Simon's pile.

The following morning the two brothers met and walked together to work, each smiling inwardly and trying to hide the pleasure each had in store for the other. Imagine their complete surprise when they discovered that both stacks of barley sheaves were exactly the same!

Neither of them said anything, they simply threw themselves into the work in hand. They were thus occupied all day long and it was only later on that Menasseh and Simon separately decided to repeat their secret work under cover of nightfall.

At daybreak the following morning the same thing happened. As soon as they arrived at their

field they saw immediately that the sheaves remained divided exactly in half.

Simon made up his mind to investigate. That night instead of going to bed he hurried back to the field as soon as it was dark. He moved his sheaves on to Menasseh's pile as quickly as he could and, carefully hiding himself, sat down to wait. Not long afterwards he made out the familiar form of his brother approaching. As soon as Menasseh started moving his own sheaves on to Simon's heap, Simon understood what had been happening. He called out to Menasseh and they hugged each other and laughed together and then wept for joy. They thanked God for giving each of them a true and generous brother.

And it is said that God blessed that place where the brothers had thought their worthy thoughts, where their good deeds were enacted, and where their tears of joy had fallen. And King Solomon chose that very spot on which to build the Holy Temple.

Legends from the Middle Ages

The Middle Ages is a term used by historians to denote the period of European history which falls between the ancient and modern worlds. Although precise dates cannot be given to its beginning and end, it is generally agreed that the Middle Ages began in the fifth century of the Common Era, after the fall of the Roman Empire, and lasted until the middle of the fifteenth century. Towards the end of this long period the Renaissance—a French word meaning 'Rebirth'—gave new meaning and importance to cultural life.

But long before the Renaissance, the early centuries of the Middle Ages were times of confusion, often known as the Dark Ages, when the influence of Roman civilization was abandoned and a period of cultural and economic decline set in.

For the Jews, who had been driven from their homeland and dispersed throughout Europe, conditions varied at different places and at different times. For example, for the Jews who lived in Spain the period between the tenth and thirteenth centuries was a so-called 'Golden Age'. At that time comparative tolerance was shown towards them and they were able to make a great contribution to literature, philosophy and medicine.

Later on, however, the Jewish people became the victims of severe religious and economic oppression throughout most of Europe. They were forced to live in walled ghettos which were built in the poorest sections of the towns. They were restricted to the most menial trades, and communication with their Gentile neighbours was made more difficult by the fact that the Jews spoke their own language. The result was that for about two hundred and fifty years they were cut off from and deprived of the rapid cultural developments which were taking place in the outside world. It was the Emperor Napoleon in his military campaigns in Europe following the French Revolution who unlocked the gates of the ghettos and brought a measure of liberty to the Jewish communities.

Meanwhile life in the ghetto was governed by religious devotion and a strict code of morality. The poor overcrowded conditions were compensated, to a certain extent, by a growth of folk tales and stories many of which attempted to portray a happier life than the one the Jews were actually experiencing.

The stories told in those days were peopled with a rich variety of figures who defended Jewish life—God, the rabbis, and the Golem; and a range of enemies—the Angel of Death, evil viziers and priests, giants and demons. Many of the stories relied on the most secret Name of God—a symbol of God Himself, which was used as a powerful protection against all enemies. But the underlying theme of these tales—which stretch from fantasy to enlightenment—was to point a moral purpose and to encourage the reader, or indeed the listener, for many of these tales were told and retold, to keep the Jewish faith alive in order to merit a place in paradise—the world to come.

The pious ox

There was once a God-fearing Jewish farmer who was the proud owner of a fine strong ox. They made a good team ploughing the fields together. Through no fault of his own the man fell on hard times and lost all his money. When he had used up his savings he was forced to sell both his farm and his ox. The new owner, a Gentile, was pleased with his purchase and all went well at first. For six days the ox pulled the plough willingly enough, but on the seventh day he just lay down and refused to work. The owner was astonished at the ox's behaviour. Neither coaxing nor beating had any effect on the animal. In spite of the frustration and fury of his new master the ox would not move an inch. In despair the Gentile went to the Jewish farmer to see if he could solve this strange mystery.

'I am most dissatisfied,' the ox's new owner told the Jewish farmer. 'I did not realize what a bad bargain I had made when I bought your ox. The strange thing is that he worked so well for the last six days without any trouble at all. But today, no matter how hard I whip him, he stubbornly refuses to move.'

The pious Jew understood immediately what had happened. The animal, like his first master, had become accustomed to resting on the seventh day of the week—the Sabbath.

'Leave it to me,' he told the Gentile, 'I will make him work.' He walked up to the ox and gently whispered in his ear: 'When I owned you we both worked hard together during the week and rested on the Sabbath day. When I could no longer afford to run my farm I had to sell you to this Gentile who seems ignorant of the sacredness of the Holy Sabbath. Please obey your new master and work for him whenever he asks you.'

As soon as the Jewish farmer had finished speaking the ox stood up and walked towards the fields. The Gentile could barely hide his astonishment. 'Whatever did you whisper to the ox?' he said. 'Have you bewitched it? I demand to know your secret.'

The pious Jew patiently explained the reason for the ox's strange behaviour and what he had said to him. The Gentile was amazed when he heard what had happened. 'Here is a simple animal without speech or reason,' he said, 'and yet it acknowledges the God of the Universe and rests on the Sabbath day. How can I, who have been created in God's image, ignore His commandments?' He was so impressed that he converted to Judaism and spent the rest of his life studying God's Holy Law.

Many years later, he became a famous teacher, known as Rabbi Jochanan of Bartotha.

The fox's heart

The Holy One spoke to the Angel of Death, saying: 'Take a pair of every kind of creature and throw them into the sea. You will then have power over all the remaining animals of that species.' The Angel of Death was quick to obey God's command, for he realized that if he did so, he would control the destiny of every living thing to the end of time.

But there was no fooling the cunning fox. He saw immediately what was happening and planned accordingly. He started to wail and howl in a most pitiful manner.

'Why are you crying like that?' the Angel of Death asked him.

'You have drowned my companions, is that not sufficient cause to weep?' the fox replied.

'Where are they?' asked the Angel, who did not

remember very clearly which animals he had already dealt with.

'Come with me and I will show you,' said the fox and he ran off and stood close to the edge of the sea. There the Angel of Death saw the reflection of a fox in the water, and he naturally presumed this was the body of one of a pair of foxes he had thrown into the sea.

'Be off with you!' he shouted. The fox did not need to be told twice. He ran until he reached the safety of his lair. There he lay panting, extremely relieved to have saved his own skin by such a clever ruse.

Later, the fox met the weasel and told him what had happened. The weasel listened intently, followed the fox's example to the letter, and he too managed to save his own life.

All the animals that the Angel of Death threw into the sea became the prisoners of Leviathan, King of the Fishes. There were so many different kinds that it was only at the end of the year that he discovered that both the fox and the weasel were missing from his collection. He was most upset when he heard how these animals had escaped their fate by tricking the Angel of Death. The other creatures were scornful.

'Surely you must have heard about the exploits of the cunning fox?' they mocked.

Something had to be done, and without delay. Leviathan sent for a school of big fish and bellowed, 'I cannot allow the fox to lead a free and independent life when all the other species are my prisoners here. Bring him to me at once—I do not care what methods you use—fair or foul. Deceive him in any way you wish, but do not fail to capture him.' The fishes needed no second bidding and swam off in search of their prey.

They soon caught sight of the fox playing by the seashore. They diverted him with a fine aquatic display—leaping into the air and diving into the water again. The inquisitive fox came nearer for a better view.

'Who are you?' the fishes paused to ask.

'I am the fox,' he replied.

'Of course, the fox. Have you not heard the news?' they asked.

'News? What news?' asked the fox.

'As a matter of a fact it's about you,' they teased.

The fox was becoming irritated: 'How on earth can that be?' he snapped.

'We have been sent to tell you of a great honour that awaits you,' they announced.

The fox was flattered although he tried to appear unconcerned. 'I cannot possibly imagine what kind of honour is intended,' he said. 'Unfortunately, Leviathan, King of the Fishes, is very sick and on the point of death. He must have a successor and he is so impressed with your reputation for wisdom and prudence that he has appointed you to reign in his place.' They waited for a moment to see how the fox would react, then went on. 'We will be honoured to be your special messengers and take you to Leviathan.'

'But I cannot swim and there is no way to reach Leviathan without my being drowned,' the fox argued.

'Nonsense, we can easily overcome that problem,' the fishes hastily assured him. 'All you have to do is to climb on the back of the biggest fish, and he will carry you over the waves. It will be such a smooth journey you won't even get your feet wet and before you know it you will be the new ruler of Leviathan's kingdom.'

The fox was finally convinced and, without a backward glance, he jumped on to the back of the biggest fish. But no sooner had they reached the open sea and the first big wave washed over him, than the fox realized that he had been well and truly deceived.

His mind raced. 'My vanity was my downfall, and I have no one to blame but myself. It was such a clever trick, it was almost worthy to be one of my own!' he thought ruefully. 'But time is running out and I must find a way to escape before I perish.' Then, he spoke to the fish who was carrying him. 'You have fooled me and no mistake, but what will happen to me now?'

There was a delicate pause and then the fish said, 'These are Leviathan's exact words: Because the fox is famous for his wisdom, I will kill him, remove his heart and eat it, so that I too can become as wise as he.'

'Stop! Stop! Did you say heart?' the fox called out. 'You should have told me before so that I could have brought my heart with me and presented it to Leviathan. In that way he would become wise like me, and I would have been honoured for my gift. I am afraid there will be trouble if you arrive without it,' and he laid emphasis on the word 'trouble'.

'What do you mean? Where is your heart?' the fish asked nervously.

'Did you not know that foxes always lock their hearts away until they are needed? It would not be fitting to use such a precious organ every day! After all I was only playing when you came for me.'

All the fishes heard the fox's words and they gathered around to discuss this worrying new development. 'What do you think we should do?' they asked.

'My lair is quite near the seashore and you can take me there and wait until I have collected my heart and then we will return together. Just imagine our triumphant entry! I will present my heart to the king who will reward us handsomely.' And the fox pressed the point home again: 'But if we go without it, it will be too late to explain how I offered to go back and fetch it. A new deputation of fishes will be sent to escort me—and you will. . .' and he paused for effect, 'you will no doubt make a hearty meal for the King of the Fishes.'

The last remark removed any last remaining doubts. Without a moment's hesitation the fishes turned round and swam back to the shore. The fox leaped on to the sand, shook himself thoroughly, and then rolled on his back in sheer ecstasy.

'Hurry, hurry!' the fishes called out from the sea, 'be quick and get your heart and come back with us.'

'Go yourselves, you silly, stupid fishes,' the fox taunted from the safety of the shore. 'How could I or any other living creature possibly survive without a heart?'

'We should have known you were lying,' they moaned. 'We have been tricked.'

'Of course you have,' the fox replied. 'Fools! I outwitted the Angel of Death—and though it was touch and go, I finally got the better of a school of feather-brained fishes.' And with that the fox disappeared from sight.

Reluctantly the fishes returned and shamefacedly confessed everything to Leviathan who told them, 'The plain facts are that the fox is cunning and you are foolish. What a pity you didn't take more notice of that saying from the Book of Proverbs: When the simpleton does not listen he comes to grief, and the stupid are ruined by their own complacency.'

'But it is too late for you to heed its warning,' the Leviathan said as he swallowed them all up.

The clever thief

There was once a hard-working man who fell on hard times. He was unable to find work and was forced to live off his meagre savings, until little by little he had pawned or sold everything he owned. The day came when he had to face the stark reality of his situation. He was penniless, hungry and forced to beg for food to keep body and soul together.

One day he went to a busy market in the hope of finding work or, if that failed, to beg a few coins to buy some bread. But no one wanted to hire him and no one gave him charity. Then he came to a stall piled high with hot meat pies. The delicious smell of freshly baked pastry was irresistible and the poor man almost fainted with hunger. He looked around and as there was no one looking after the stall, he quickly grabbed a pie and ate it greedily. At that very moment the stallholder returned, caught the poor man in the act and charged him with stealing. He was taken to prison, convicted of theft and ordered to be hanged.

On the way to the gallows, the poor man told the prison warder that he had inherited a most wonderful secret from his late father. 'Alas, I have no son to pass it on to, and it would be a great pity to let it die with me. Will you grant me a last wish and ask the king if he would honour me by accepting my secret as a gift?'

The prison warder listened sympathetically, and mentioned the matter to the prison governor who in turn informed the king. At first the king dismissed the idea, but gradually his interest was aroused and he ordered the convicted man to appear before him.

'What is the nature of this wonderful secret you wish to share with me?' he asked.

The poor man explained. 'I will plant a pomegranate seed and then, using a magic formula my father taught me, I will make it grow into a tree which will bear fruit—all within the space of twenty-four hours!'

The king was now full of curiosity and, accompanied by his grand vizier and high-ranking officers, he arranged to meet the convicted man the following day. When they arrived at the appointed place they watched carefully as the ground was prepared. 'Your Majesty and honourable gentlemen,' began the prisoner. 'As you can see, the earth is ready and here is the pomegranate seed. I must, however, mention that it can only be sown by a man who has never in his life stolen, or taken anything—not even the smallest trifle—which did not belong to him. As I have been convicted of theft, I am naturally disqualified from this task.' And he offered the pomegranate seed to the king. 'Sire, I would be most honoured if you would plant this seed.'

The king hesitated, then he suggested that the vizier might act on his behalf.

The vizier looked embarrassed. 'When I was a young man I borrowed my friend's fine cloak—to impress a young lady, you understand—and I never returned it,' he confessed.

On the king's instruction the seed was offered next to the chancellor of the exchequer. He, too, looked rather shamefaced. 'The problem is that when dealing with large sums of money it is easy to make entries in the book-keeping ledgers of either too much. . .' he coughed, 'or too little money.'

The poor man offered the seed to the king once more, and now even he confessed to having once taken one of his father's rings. 'He had so much jewellery, I did not think he would miss it,' he added lamely.

Still holding the pomegranate seed, the poor man plucked up courage and spoke out: 'Respected gentlemen, you are all wealthy men and hold positions of great power, yet none of you is eligible to sow this seed because of some minor petty theft. As for me, I stole a meat pie because I was starving to death, and for that I am to be hanged.'

The king was both affected and impressed with the convicted man's clever defence and it was with great pleasure that he granted him a royal pardon.

The plucked pigeon

Daniel the Jew hated the winter weather, especially when he had to wash the sheep's wool before sending it to market. It was a thankless job, and to make matters worse the water in the creek was icy cold.

One day as Daniel was working and bemoaning the fact that his fingers were numb with cold, the sultan and his attendants chanced to ride by.

'Tell me,' the sultan asked Daniel, 'which is greater—five or seven?'

Daniel stood up, bowed low to the sultan and answered his riddle with one of his own: 'Which is greater—twelve or thirty-two?'

The sultan nodded, but chose not to answer Daniel directly. Instead he tried him with another puzzle. 'Have you ever had a fire in your house?' he asked him.

'Yes, your honour, I have had five fires, and I have reason to believe that there will be two more,' Daniel replied.

The sultan seemed satisfied with this response, then with a wry grin he asked him: 'If I send you one of my pigeons, will you be able to pluck it?'

'If you send one to me, you will be able to see for yourself.' Daniel answered.

While this strange dialogue was going on, the members of the sultan's household listened in amazement, but did not dare to interrupt. Then the sultan turned to his vizier and asked: 'Did you understand anything of the conversation between myself and the Jew?'

The vizier was irritated. 'How could I possibly have known what you were talking about—after all you were speaking in riddles,' he retorted.

'Indeed! Well you do surprise me,' the sultan replied mockingly. 'Let me remind you that as the holder of the high position of vizier you are supposed to be the wisest man in the land next to me. Whereas a simple Jew was able to understand me, you, it seems, were not. I will give you just three days to produce the correct answers, otherwise you will be dismissed.' And the sultan rode off with his retinue following at a respectful distance.

The vizier was visibly shocked by the sultan's unexpected pronouncement. He hurried back to his palace and called a meeting of the wisest counsellors and repeated to them the riddles which the sultan had asked Daniel. They sat in the library studying learned volumes, discussing at length every turn of phrase, trying to find the hidden message in the numbers and words—but without success. No matter how long and hard he concentrated on the problem, the vizier found himself back where he had started. And time was passing. In the end he pocketed his pride and sent his servant to bring Daniel the Jew to his palace.

'Tell me, what is the meaning of the riddles which the sultan set for you?' he asked Daniel. 'The price of the information you need is one thousand dinars,' Daniel replied.

The vizier was furious. 'You have the audacity to expect me to pay a small fortune for explaining the significance of a few ridiculous sentences!' he stormed.

Daniel spoke with quiet dignity. 'If it is not worth the money, you are under no obligation to pay me,' and he bowed low, left the palace and returned home.

But when, inevitably, the morning of the third day arrived, the vizier was still no nearer a solution. In a state of panic and fear he sent his messenger a second time to bring Daniel to the palace as quickly as possible. As soon as Daniel arrived he was rushed before the vizier who was waiting with ill-concealed impatience.

The vizier handed Daniel a package. 'Here, take this—one thousand dinars—and now kindly interpret the riddles for me.' And the vizier waited impatiently to hear what Daniel had to say.

Daniel put the money into his pocket,

thanked the vizier and began: 'When the sultan saw me washing wool in the icy stream he asked me which was the bigger number, five or seven. The hidden meaning behind these two numbers was this. The sultan wished to know whether I earned enough during the seven warm months of the year to make it unnecessary for me to work during the five cold months. I answered that thirty-two was more than twelve. By this I implied that with my thirty-two teeth I would eat more food than I could buy with what I could earn in twelve months.

'The sultan then asked me whether I had ever had a fire in my house. He merely wished to know whether I had married off any of my children, for when a person has finished paying all the expenses of a wedding, he is cleaned out financially, so to speak, and left as destitute as if his house had burned down. I told him that I had already had five fires and there were still two more to come.

'And lastly the sultan asked me whether, if he were to send me one of his pigeons, I would be able to pluck it.' Turning to the vizier he said: 'Sire, you heard my reply to the sultan. I told him: Just send one along to me, and you will see! Perhaps you would be kind enough to go to the sultan and ask him whether I have succeeded or not!'

Asking for the impossible

There was once a cruel and powerful ruler who gave his Jewish subjects good cause to fear and hate him, for they were constantly discriminated against and oppressed without mercy. The king was a wastrel, a spendthrift, and an incurable gambler. He was always looking for new ways of raising money to replenish the royal coffers.

One day the king issued a proclamation ordering the Jews to raise an enormous sum of money in a short time. As if that were not enough, he sent an ultimatum which stated that if they failed to carry out his order within the time allowed they would be expelled from his kingdom.

The news of this dreadful edict spread like

wildfire throughout the Jewish quarter. They went into deep mourning, they tore their garments, put ashes on their heads and prayed fervently to God to intercede on their behalf.

The elders of the Jewish community met together to discuss the terrible decree. The majority of them were poor merchants and well aware that it was impossible to raise anything like the amount demanded by the king, even without the additional burden of a time limit. The prospect looked bleak.

In desperation they decided to ask the help of a famous rabbi, Rabbi Isaac Luria, better known as Ari Hakodesh or the Holy Lion. This man was pious and learned and an authority on the mystical teachings of Judaism. Although he lived in Safed in the Land of Israel, his reputation had spread to eastern Europe. Everyone in the community contributed towards the cost of sending two messengers, who set sail without further delay.

Blessed with fair winds and clear nights the ship anchored safely in the port of Acre and from there the two men travelled overland to Safed. They reached the city late one Friday evening, just before the beginning of the Sabbath. Although they were very tired they did not stop to rest until they arrived at the rabbi's house.

The Holy Lion was fully prepared to greet the Sabbath. He was dressed in spotless white robes and his face shone with radiance as if he were in touch with the presence of God. His devoted disciples sat in a circle round him, listening to his wise teachings.

The rabbi welcomed the travellers warmly: 'Shalom aleichem—peace be with you. What brings you to Safed?'
'We have come a great distance to ask you to intercede with God on our behalf, to help save an entire Jewish community,' they answered, and explained in detail the nature of the wicked king's impossible demands.
'You must stay with me until the end of the Sabbath. Now go and wash and rest yourselves,' the rabbi told them. 'And while you are my guests, you must forget all your worries and problems for it is a sin to desecrate the peace of the Sabbath with sad thoughts.

Remember, God never abandons the righteous.'

The two travel-weary men were only too happy to comply with the rabbi's request. The following evening, when the blessing for the conclusion of the Sabbath had been recited, the rabbi spoke to his disciples and the messengers. 'Bring a long, strong rope with you and follow me,' he ordered. Carrying the rope between them, they followed the rabbi to a distant field, in the middle of which was a deep pit.

Then the rabbi spoke again. 'Lower the rope to the bottom and be sure to hold fast to the end.' When they had done this he called out: 'Now heave away with all your strength!'

The men pulled together with a will, wondering what the heavy weight at the rope's end could possibly be. Little by little the rope was slowly hauled to the surface. Curiosity turned to amazement as a magnificent bed gradually came into view. With a final heave, the bed stood firmly on the ground.

The men could hardly believe their eyes when they saw a king in full regalia, fast asleep on the bed. The rabbi went over to the sleeping monarch and shook him awake.
'Are you the heartless ruler who is so cruelly oppressing his Jewish subjects?' he demanded.

The king had no need to reply. The look on his face and the way he trembled in every limb were sufficient proof of his guilt.
'Get up,' the rabbi commanded, and handed the king a dipper—a ladle-shaped bowl with a handle. But this dipper was different—it was full of holes! Then he took the king to a nearby well. 'Take this dipper and empty the well,' he ordered. 'You will have to work quickly, for I want the task completed before dawn tomorrow.'

The king was horrified when he saw the hopelessness of his task. 'If I live to be a hundred years old, I could never empty the well with this useless tool,' he moaned.
'Very well. You have recognized that the job I gave you cannot possibly be achieved. Why then do you ask the poor Jews in your kingdom for something which is totally beyond their reach?'

The king began to feel remorseful. 'You are right, Rabbi, you have made me understand that my edict was both unfair and cruel. I will withdraw the order—only please spare my life,' he pleaded.

'Give me your signet ring as a token of your assurance,' demanded the rabbi. The king handed over his ring without a word of protest.

The next thing the messengers knew was that the bed, the rabbi and his disciples had all dissappeared; they were standing in the street outside their own houses.

The following morning the king's servant woke him gently. 'Good morning, Your Majesty, I trust you slept well?'

The king opened his eyes. 'No, I did not. I had a terrible dream,' he said, shuddering at the memory. Nevertheless, in spite of his efforts to blot it from his mind, the details of his dream continued to recur in vivid sequence. And when he looked at the index finger of his right hand and saw that his signet ring was missing, he knew, beyond the shadow of a doubt, that his experience had been real enough. The king did not wait for the final date set by his proclamation to arrive. Instead he called for the two messengers and gave them a signed order rescinding all demands of money from the Jews.

The two men bowed low and thanked the king profusely. One of them handed the signet ring to him. 'Your majesty, on behalf of your Jewish subjects, please accept our heartfelt thanks. Our fervent prayers to God have been answered. Rabbi Isaac Luria will be delighted to hear the good news.'

The king looked thoughtful. 'I have learned a great deal from your learned rabbi. I appreciate full well that faithful citizens deserve a king who will rule with honesty and understanding. Rest assured that I will never again make impossible demands on the Jewish community.'

The miser's transformation

Wolf Mordecai Krantz was a very rich man. He lived in the lap of luxury. He owned lands and property, and his spacious house was resplendent with all manner of beautiful ornaments, handsome rugs and the finest hand-crafted furniture that money could buy. He also had coffers, chests and boxes of all shapes and sizes full of gold and silver and precious jewels.

Wolf's only failing was that he was tight-fisted. Unlike other wealthy Jews, he persistently ignored one of the most fundamental obligations of the Jewish religion—that of giving charity. He turned a deaf ear to those in distress, and although he was well versed in the Torah, he frequently absented himself from synagogue services just to avoid being asked for a donation of money for the poor. It was hardly surprising that he earned the nickname 'the Miser'.

Nevertheless he had one redeeming quality. He was an experienced mohel—a person who circumcises newly born males according to Jewish law. He considered this task to be a mitzvah, that is, a sacred good deed, and because of this he performed the religious service free of charge, irrespective of the length of the journey he had to travel, or the time and effort involved.

One day a stranger called at his house and asked if he would circumcise his little son, who had been born a few days previously. The miser congratulated the new father. 'It would give me great pleasure to perform the holy covenant for you. Where do you live?' he asked.

'I am not a local man,' answered the stranger, 'in fact my home is a good distance from here. But you have no need to worry. I have a light carriage and good horses and they can keep up a good speed.'

'Very well,' Wolf replied, 'I will be ready to go with you in a few moments, but first I must attend to one or two matters.' Then with the thoroughness of a true miser, he carefully examined all the containers that held his gold and silver and jewels to make sure that everything was safely locked away. When he was quite satisfied he bolted the door and the gate of his house, climbed into the waiting carriage and sat down next to the stranger.

They set off at a slow, unhurried pace. The miser, comforted in the knowledge that he had left his house and possessions quite secure from the most determined burglars, sat back to enjoy the ride. Then, without warning, the stranger whipped up his horses and began to drive at

breakneck speed through woods and fields, galloping up hills and careering down the other side. On and on they went without pausing for rest until finally a mist descended, and night closed in around them.

Throughout the journey the miser was aware of an uncanny feeling which he was unable to identify. 'There is something missing, something missing,' he muttered to himself. Then, with a shudder, he realized what it was. At no time had he heard the song of a bird, or the hum of an insect—nothing. It was as if all the normal sounds of nature had been silenced.

By now the miser was beginning to feel decidedly uneasy. At last the moon came up and cast its eerie light upon the landscape. On and on they sped through the night with the carriage lurching wildly and sparks flying from the horses' hooves as they pounded the road. The miser's mouth was dry with fear. 'Where are you taking me—surely the horses must be tired by now and in need of a rest,' he said nervously.

'We have not much further to go,' the stranger assured him. And as if his words had released a hidden trigger, the dawn broke, the mist lifted and the sun shone—its brilliant rays highlighting a little hamlet nestling in a valley below them.

As they approached the village a group of men came out to welcome them: 'Shalom, shalom aleichem—peace, peace be with you,' they called out. The servants led the horses to the stable while the stranger escorted his guest into the house.

The miser could hardly believe his eyes. In all his life he had never seen anything quite like the opulence and splendour which surrounded him. It made his own fine collection seem tawdry and inferior by comparison. The furniture was inlaid with sparkling gems, there was a magnificent display of the rarest gold and silver objects, the doors were made of carved ivory and even the locks and bolts on the doors were made of gold. 'I am sure my host will offer me one of his precious objects in appreciation of my services,' he thought to himself, 'but which one?' And he continued to speculate as he wandered from room to room, each one more

lavishily decorated than the last. Finally he came to a beautiful room in the middle of which was a huge four-poster bed. Propped up on silken pillows was the young mother and, by her side, in a cradle made of pure beaten gold, her new born baby lay sleeping quietly.

The miser hesitated in the doorway until she beckoned him over to her side. 'Kind sir,' she murmured, 'I am most indebted to you for coming such a long way to perform this service for my little son. I will reward you—not with costly gifts as you might well have expected—but by sharing my secret with you.' Then she signed to him to make sure the door was closed, and continued: 'If you have already felt misgivings about this place they are, sadly, justified. There are no mortal men here apart from yourself. You are in the company of demons, including my husband who enticed you here with lies and deception. The fabulous collections of gold and gems are only a shallow sham.'

An icy stab of fear ran down Wolf's spine at these words. The young woman then told him, 'I am human like yourself, but being young and vain I became a helpless victim of the demon's evil plans. He flattered my vanity and courted me with wonderful gifts which I stupidly accepted. It all happened so quickly, and before I knew it I became the wife of a demon!'

She began to weep bitterly. The miser was on the point of offering words of comfort but she stopped him. 'Please do not waste your sympathy on me, for I am quite beyond redemption, but there is still time for me to save you. So listen carefully.
'I beg of you do not eat or drink anything at all—not even a tiny morsel of food or the merest sip of wine, however much it is pressed on you. You must be strong-minded and on your guard at all times to resist every temptation. Do not accept any gifts from my husband, irrespective of whether they are the most expensive or just a modest trifle.'

Full of fear and trepidation the miser nodded, lost for words. He felt certain he was doomed to become the demon's next victim and thought wistfully of all he had left behind. He thanked the young woman sincerely and left the room.

As soon as it was dark the miser was startled by a deafening commotion outside. Above the clatter of the wagons and horses in the courtyard, he could hear loud voices and shouts of raucous laughter. 'They must be all the demon-guests arriving for the circumcision celebration,' he said to himself, and shivered at the thought.

Once again the miser was obliged to visit the mother and child in her room, accompanied this time by his host and the rest of the demons. It was indeed a cruel irony when, in that dreadful company, he was asked to recite the prayers which would guard the child against evil spirits and ghosts!

That night the miser tossed and turned on his bed, wide awake and worried not only by what he had experienced that day, but by what might well be in store for him in the morning.

The next day he was taken to the synagogue, which was crowded with demon-worshippers, and courteously invited to lead the prayers. He read aloud one portion of the service and sang another, and each time the demons responded with their chants his soul was filled with anguish.

When the service was over, the baby was brought in and the miser successfully performed the circumcision. According to custom everyone was given a glass of wine with which to toast the child's good health. The miser excused himself on the pretext that this was his special fast day. Not to be outwitted, the demon announced. 'It is our duty to honour the mohel, so we will postpone our feast until this evening when his fast will be at an end. He will be able to participate fully in the celebrations.'

The miser's heart sank and for the rest of the day he could think of nothing but how he might refuse to take part in the feast and save his soul from the devil.

As soon as it was dark the miser was led to the great dining hall where the demons were seated at a long table piled high with dishes of aromatic and appetizing foods and flagons of the rarest wines. Everyone was in a festive mood, eating and drinking heartily. Only the miser sat in solemn slience. Each time he was offered food and drink he confessed to feeling unwell. The more the merrymaking increased, the more nervous and ill at ease he felt.

In the middle of the festivities, the demon-host rose and asked the miser to follow him. 'This might be my last moment on earth,' the terrifed miser said to himself and followed slowly and reluctantly.

They entered a room which he had not seen before. The miser was dazzled by the display of beautiful and precious objects, some encrusted with gems, others patterned with finely worked silver.
'As a token of my appreciation for your service to my little son, I would be pleased if you would choose a gift from among my treasures,' the demon declared.

Although he was frightened, the miser did not forget what he must do. He thought quickly and replied, 'Thank you most kindly for your generous offer, but it has always been my practice to perform a circumcision free of charge. I cannot, therefore, accept any gift.'

Without a word the demon led him into a second room, and pointed to more exquisite articles, this time made of pure gold. 'Perhaps you would care to select something here?' he suggested. It was a tantalizing decision to make but the miser remained steadfast. 'Thank you again, but the same rule applies. I cannot accept any gift,' he repeated, trying hard to look indifferent to the treasures around him.

The demon frowned but said nothing. Then he took the miser to a third room. There were no magnificent objects here, no glitter and sparkle of precious jewels, no bright glow of gold. Instead the walls were lined from floor to ceiling with row upon row of hooks from which hung bunches of keys of all shapes and sizes and all made from a common base metal. The miser was relieved not to be tempted by this collection and allowed himself to look at it closely.
'Well, well!' the demon remarked. 'How strange that my treasures of gold and silver had no effect on you, and yet you show a keen interest in a collection of old keys.'

But what had begun as a pleasure soon turned to deadly fear, for immediately opposite him the miser saw a familiar bunch of keys—his own! 'I think those are my keys,' he gasped. He stepped forward to take a closer look. 'I recognize them,' and his voice dropped to a frightened whisper, 'as the ones that fit the locks of my coffers and chests.'

'I know that. Now pay attention to what I have to say. I am a demon—the all-powerful lord and master of all the evil spirits who wield power over the treasured possessions of miserly human beings like yourself. You who care only for the accumulation of possessions and wealth and nothing for the poor and needy.' The miser turned grey, but the demon continued. 'Just remember this, although you think you own your boxes of treasures, we demons hold the keys and guard them very well, even though we can never enjoy them. But you did me a great service and refused to accept any reward for it. I will show my appreciation by giving you your bunch of keys.'

The miser stopped trembling just long enough to snatch his keys. Then the carriage was ordered and he climbed up beside the driver, who drove them away. Throughout the return journey the miser sat with his head in his hands and only looked up when the horses came to a standstill outside his house. As soon as his feet touched the ground the driver, the carriage and the horses vanished into thin air.

From that moment on the miser was transformed. It is true that he unlocked all his chests and boxes to see if the keys he had been given worked, but the contents had lost all their attraction. He was no longer mean and selfish—in fact the nickname of 'the Miser' was soon dropped, never to be recalled. Wolf became well known for his generosity and hospitality which he showed to friend and stranger alike. The door to his house was always open and no one in need was ever turned away empty handed. And for the first time in his life he experienced a deep and lasting satisfaction and a feeling of contentment which continued to his dying day.

He would have been truly delighted had he been able to witness his own funeral. On that occasion the entire town turned out and followed his coffin to honour the man who had a change of heart.

The golem of Prague

The word 'golem' is only mentioned once in the Bible, but in the Talmud it has come to mean lifeless, shapeless matter, something unformed and imperfect—a kind of body without a soul.

A golem was a human-looking creature which was made by an act of magic through the use of holy names. The idea that it was possible to create living beings in this manner was not a unique invention of the Jews, but common in the magic lore of many other peoples. Jewish folklore gives many accounts of rabbis who not only created golems but returned them to dust when they were no longer required. Most of them were used as attendants or bodyguards, and whereas they were supposed to have been able to understand and follow commands, they lacked the power of speech—a gift which God alone could grant.

During the Middle Ages legends about the golem became widespread among the Jews of eastern Europe. The famous Rabbi Elijah of Chelm is reputed to have created a golem by writing God's Holy Name on a piece of parchment and sticking it on the forehead of a clay model of a man. Not for one moment did it occur to the rabbi that he might be creating a monster that would run amok destroying everything in its path. When the golem proved uncontrollable Rabbi Elijah had no choice but to remove the parchment from its forehead, whereupon it immediately turned to dust.

The middle of the seventeenth century was marked by one of the worst periods of persecution of the Jews. The root cause was the spreading of deliberate lies and trumped-up allegations that Jews murdered non-Jews, especially Christians, in order to obtain blood for the Passover or other rituals. These blood libels became an excuse for the most terrible attacks on innocent people. The widespread massacres left the Jewish communities decimated and shattered.

To be locked away in poor, overcrowded ghettos was hard enough, but the feeling that God had abandoned them was an intolerable burden for them to bear. It was little wonder, therefore, that the magical figure of the golem became such an important part of Jewish folklore. With its great physical strength, its supernatural power to unearth the evil plots of their enemies, the golem became a kind of imagined redeemer to the Jews, helping them to cope with the daily problem of survival. By far the most popular of all the golem stories are those told about the Golem of Prague.

Rabbi Yehuda Lowe of Prague was a learned, pious man known as the Maharal, a term formed from the initial letters of the Hebrew words which mean: 'Our teacher the master Rabbi Lowe'. He was a renowned scholar of the Torah and the Talmud, a wise counsellor in the settling of disputes, an excellent teacher of young and old alike, and a gifted storyteller.

Rabbi Lowe's learning was not confined to rabbinical studies. He was an eminent scholar and could speak several languages fluently. The Maharal was highly regarded by scholars in both the Jewish and Gentile communities and was even granted an audience with King Rudolf of Bohemia—a great honour.

The Jewish community of Prague took great pride in their famous rabbi. They knew he worked tirelessly to silence the enemies who continually plotted their destruction. There was a feeling of relief and joy when the rabbi received assurances from the king himself that the blood accusations and brutal killing of innocent Jews would no longer be permitted.

One night the Maharal had a vivid dream in which he found himself in the Christian quarter of the city. There, to his horror, he witnessed a terrible crime in which a child was killed, its body placed in a sack, and taken to a house in the Jewish ghetto. The Maharal recognized the murderer as none other than the evil Thaddeus, a priest whose sole aim was to destroy the Jews. As the festival of Passover was approaching, the rabbi realized that the Jews as a whole would be blamed for this crime which would start yet another wave of false accusations and savage attacks. He prayed for help and the answer came immediately. In his dream he saw the most sacred Name of God and a formula of mystical words which he was able to decipher. It read: 'Create a golem out of clay who will

destroy the enemies of Israel.' Before he had a chance to question further, Rabbi Lowe awoke.

The rabbi was overwhelmed by the effects of his powerful dream. Its meaning was clear and he knew he must act quickly for, despite the king's pledge, he saw that the dream's message carried a grave warning of a new plot against his people.

He went straight to the house of his son-in-law Isaac, and his trusted disciple Jacob, woke them up and told them to dress quickly. The three walked in silence through the darkness to the bank of the River Moldau.

When they arrived the rabbi took Isaac and Jacob into his confidence. He described his dream and swore them to secrecy about his plans. The Maharal knew that he could create a golem using the mystical secrets hidden in the Hebrew word-formula.

The men set to work and dug a large quantity of clay which the Maharal skilfully shaped into a man of immense size. Then he fashioned hands, feet and a head and drew its features with great care. When everything was completed to his satisfaction, Rabbi Lowe took a piece of parchment from his pocket on which he had written God's most Holy Name and placed it in the mouth of the clay figure. Then he walked round it, seven times in one direction and seven times in the opposite direction, at the same time chanting mystical incantations.

The three men looked on in amazement for no sooner had this been completed than the clay figure began to glow like fire. Then the Maharal recited a magical formula that had never before been pronounced. Finally, the three men recited together the passage from the Book of Genesis: 'And he breathed into his nostrils the breath of life; and man became a living soul.' At that moment the irridescent light disappeared, the clay figure sat up, opened his eyes and looked wonderingly at the Maharal.
'Get up on your feet!' ordered the Maharal. The figure obeyed instantly and put on the clothes the men had brought with them.
'This is a golem whom we will call Joseph,' the Rabbi explained to Isaac and Jacob. 'Although he cannot speak he has been sent to protect us from the evil Thaddeus.' And they returned to

the town, each silently marvelling that whereas three men who had set out that night, four men were returning!

On the way back the Maharal spoke to the golem. 'You have been created to protect the defenceless Jews against their enemies. Your name is Joseph and you will serve me as a shammes—attendant—in the synagogue. You must obey me no matter what you are called upon to do.'

Although Joseph could not speak he nodded vigorously, making it plain that he understood what was expected of him.

As soon as they were home Rabbi Lowe introduced the golem to his wife Perele. 'This is Joseph,' he said. 'I found him wandering in the street and took pity on him and decided to bring him home. As you can see he cannot speak but seems to understand everything I say. He can live with us and make himself useful attending the services in the synagogue and carrying out the duties of a shammes.' Then he gave his wife a solemn warning. 'I forbid you to give Joseph any menial jobs to do in the house—the work he does must be of a holy nature,' he said.

As soon as the two men were alone the rabbi told Joseph exactly what he had seen in his dream. 'We have no time to lose,' he said gravely, 'the evil Thaddeus has the perfect excuse for another vicious attack. We can only stop him if you find the child's body.'

Joseph nodded his head and set off with great strides round the ghetto, followed by the Maharal, almost running to keep up. Joseph looked carefully at every dwelling as he went along, until at last he stopped outside a house close to the ghetto gates. The Maharal knocked on the door.

The owner, an old pious Jew, welcomed the Maharal and his strange companion. The rabbi came straight to the point. 'Learned friend, is there a cellar in this house?' he asked.
'Why, yes, there is,' the old man answered in surprise, 'but it is dank and musty and I never go down there.'

The old man led them down to the cellar and there, sure enough, was the sack exactly as the Rabbi had dreamed.

At that very moment there was a loud knocking on the door above them and the harsh voices of the guards could be heard demanding entry. While the old man climbed back up the cellar steps to open the door, the Maharal spoke urgently to Joseph. 'Thaddeus must have informed the police about the murder and told them where to search,' he said. The golem nodded and indicated that he understood the dangerous situation they were in.

Motioning the rabbi to follow, Joseph walked quickly to a dark corner at the far end of the cellar. He knelt down and pressed hard on one of the flagstones which slowly revolved to reveal a hidden staircase. Then he picked up the sack, descended the steps, and as soon as the rabbi was safely down, he pushed the flagstone back in place.

They found themselves in a maze of tunnels beneath the ghetto and leading far beyond into other parts of the city. The rabbi followed the golem along countless twists and turns of the labyrinth. until they came to a flight of stone steps, ending in what looked like a blank wall. Joseph did not hesitate for a moment but pushed with all his great strength against the wall until he had made a hole big enough for them to climb through. They found themselves in another cellar which the rabbi at once realized belonged to Thaddeus, for he could hear the priest's unmistakable voice above them. They left the sack in the cellar and returned as quickly as they could, pausing only long enough for Joseph to replace the bricks.

By the time they had returned to the house of the old pious Jew, the guards had completed their thorough search and had left empty-handed. Rabbi Lowe and the golem went to see the captain of the guards.
'It has come to my knowledge,' said the rabbi, 'that a horrible murder has been committed, and that the victim—a child—can be found in Thaddeus's cellar.'
'Come now, Rabbi,' sneered the captain, 'you can hardly expect me to believe such a wild accusation against Thaddeus.'
The captain was about to dismiss the rabbi but the sight of the golem towering silently above him with an ugly expression on his face

made him change his mind very quickly. 'Very well, I will have Thaddeus's house searched,' he snarled, 'but if there is nothing to be found, you will be charged instead and put in prison. Follow me.'

Thaddeus was visibly shocked to see the rabbi and the golem arrive with the guards. He was all bluff and bluster before the search began, but it was a different story when the child's body was discovered in his cellar. The proof of his terrible crime was plain for all to see and he was at once accused of murder.

And so the evil Thaddeus was punished, and with the help of Rabbi Lowe and the golem, the Jews of Prague were spared.

With the golem's help, life became easier for the Jews of Prague. His tall, powerful figure stood head and shoulders above anyone else and it would have been a brave man indeed who would think of taking on his towering strength. There was no need for Joseph to be on duty all the time during this quiet period. There was just a regular night watch and daily services in the synagogue to attend, after which Joseph was free to spend the rest of the day sitting on a bench in front of Rabbi Lowe's house.

Perele, the rabbi's wife, was irritated beyond measure by the sight of the golem lounging about while she was busy from dawn to late at night. She had seven children to care for to say nothing of running a busy household. Perele was sorely tempted to make use of Joseph to help her around the house, but the Rabbi had told his wife in no uncertain terms: 'Do not, on any account, give the golem any housework to do.'

His wife could not see any justification for this order and considered it to be grossly unfair.

The Jewish festival of Passover was approaching and Perele was busy with the special preparations needed to make the household ready for the eight-day festival. Rabbi Lowe's house echoed to the sound of frantic preparations. The floors had to be swept and scrubbed, all traces of leavened bread removed, Passover dishes unpacked and washed, to say nothing of the baking of special Passover food. And in the midst of all this activity there was the golem sitting idly around.

It was enough to try the patience of Job. 'I have had enough of this,' Perele said to herself. 'God knows I have never once asked the golem to help—surely my husband could not possibly object on this occasion.'

She called Joseph and gave him two buckets. 'I am going to the market and while I am gone I want you to bring water from the well and fill the two big barrels in the pantry. Do you understand?' she asked. The golem nodded, and as soon as Perele had left, he took a bucket in each hand and hurried outside to the well.

Perele's mind was now at rest. 'At least I will be spared some of the really heavy work,' she said to herself, and with that she was soon lost among the market stalls.

Later when she returned laden with shopping, she was astonished by the sight which confronted her. Jostling for the best view, a huge crowd had gathered outside their house shouting: 'A flood! A flood!' as they watched a steady stream of water pouring out of the door.

When she had managed to push her way through to the front, Perele gazed dumbfounded at the scene before her. The golem appeared, soaked to the skin and, oblivious to the fact that the barrels were full and overflowing, he dashed into the house, emptied both buckets of water, turned round and made straight for the well again, intent on repeating the process.

It was sheer good fortune which brought Rabbi Lowe home from the synagogue at that moment. He understood the situation at once and shouted: 'Joseph, stop bringing water.' The golem stopped dead, left the buckets where they stood, and splashed his way back to his bench as if nothing unusual had happened.

Rabbi Lowe then turned to the crowd and told them: 'God sent a flood to punish mankind for his sins, but this is merely a reprimand for my disobedient wife.'

When everyone had gone home the rabbi spoke to Perele privately. 'In the same way that holy vessels which are set aside for sacred purposes should never be put to everyday use, so the golem must not be used for anything except God's work.'

It took Perele, the rabbi's wife, a long time to live down the episode of the golem and the flood. From then on she was careful not to ask him to do any work in the house. Fortunately, her children were growing up fast and willingly helped their mother with the household tasks.

Some time later there was great excitement in the Lowe household. As was the custom in those days a marriage had been arranged between the rabbi's eldest daughter and the son of a rabbi from a nearby town. There was great excitement and happiness, and plans were soon under way for the wedding celebrations.

What a hive of activity—what hustle and bustle! There were relatives and friends to welcome, a wedding feast to prepare and a thousand and one details to attend to. Even with the cheerful assistance of her daughters, there were just not enough hours in the day to cope with the amount of work involved. As usual the only one with time on his hands was the golem. He sat in a corner, gazing into space, totally unaware of the feverish preparations going on around him.

Then Perele had an idea. Although her husband had expressly forbidden her to use Joseph to do menial tasks, he had told her often enough that the golem could be safely employed in pious deeds. 'But surely there is nothing more appropriate than this wedding—a match made in heaven—for Joseph to help me with?' she thought, and it did not take her long to convince herself that on this occasion it was perfectly in order for the golem to work for her.

'Joseph, I need you to help with the shopping,' Perele told him. 'Go to the market, buy a large fish and bring it back here. Do you understand?' she asked, handing Joseph some money and a note for the fisherman. Joseph nodded and set off in the direction of the river. He gave the stallholder the note and paid him, and received in turn a huge freshly-caught carp. He was very pleased with his purchase and hurried back to the house. But the fish was a slippery customer and time and again slithered out of his hands. Joseph was puzzled, then he tried another method of carrying the fish home. He placed it, head first, down his shirt front.

That worked for a while until the huge carp, far from dead, started thrashing about and dealt Joseph a powerful stinging blow across his face with its tail, which sent him reeling. That was too much. He lost his temper, jerked the fish out of his shirt, and with a mighty hurl, threw it back in the river.

Perele was furious when Joseph returned empty handed. 'Where is my fish?' she shouted. He had no words to explain. But by the time he had mimed the sequence of events, Perele understood only too clearly what had happened. 'Well,' she said in a resigned tone, 'I have no choice but to go and buy another fish.'

Then Perele remembered an errand she had forgotten all about. 'Now listen carefully, Joseph. In order to save precious time, I want you to go and buy some apples.' And once again she gave him some coins and a note explaining what she wanted.

The golem set off a second time for the market, and gave the note and the money to the stallholder who weighed the apples, put them in a bag and handed it to him. But the golem continued to stand there, as if uncertain what to do next.

'Well,' said the woman rudely, 'what are you looking for now? Haven't you got enough? Perhaps you can use these as well?' she added sarcastically, pointing to the apples piled high on the stall.

Joseph beamed and nodded his head several times. Then with a mighty heave he lifted up the entire stall, complete with the apples and the woman, placed it on his head and marched off, ignoring the loud shrieks of the terrified stallholder who was clinging to the top of the pile of fruit, and the shower of apples that rained down on his head. He puffed and panted under the weight of his burden and by the time he reached the rabbi's house he was followed by a delighted crowd, shouting and laughing as they collected the fallen apples.

Rabbi Lowe comforted the poor apple woman as best he could with some financial compensation and an invitation to the wedding feast. As for Perele, the rabbi's wife, she finally learned her lesson: that was the very last time she ever made use of the golem's services!

Rabbis and miracles

In the later years of the Renaissance, while artistic and scientific discoveries were making great advances in the western world, the Jews, suffering from hunger, poverty and persecution, were growing culturally weaker. Their lives were filled with superstition, excessive piety and the strange shadowy world of the Cabbala or Jewish mysticism.

With the rise of the popular mystical sect known as the Hasidim, which means 'God-fearing people' or 'the Pious', Cabbala took on a more joyful meaning. The earlier forbidding terrors of unspeakable demons and ghosts disappeared and in their place came the belief that one of the best ways to worship God was to read and tell wonderful tales about the *Tzaddikim*, the great rabbinical teachers. In addition it was considered that God could best be served through happiness and joy and by singing religious songs.

The founder of the Hasidic movement was Rabbi Israel, son of Eliezer—known as the Baal Shem Tov which means 'Master of the Good Name', or 'Miracle worker'. He was born in Poland and earned his living digging clay in the Carpathian mountains. There he learned about medicinal herbs and later travelled from place to place earning a reputation for being able to cure all kinds of diseases, using not only herbs, but also charms and prayer. He was well known as a storyteller, gave advice and guidance, and gradually collected a large following of disciples called *Hasidim*. They were strongly influenced by his way of life, his love of the countryside, and the importance of devout prayer. He told them that laughter, song and dance were the highest forms of prayer. To perform a *mitzvah*, a sacred good deed, was, he taught, more important than the details of rabbinical law and ritual.

The old-style rabbis who depended on charity to support them and spent their whole lives in the study of the Talmud and Torah, acquiring religious knowledge for its own sake, were remote from the ordinary Jews. Because of this the leaders of the Hasidic movement attracted thousands of simple Jewish workers whose long working hours left little time to spend on study. They had absolute faith in the Rebbes, their spiritual leaders, whom they believed were closer to God than ordinary folk, and were thus enabled to act as mediators between God and the believer. To their founder, the Baal Shem Tov, they attributed all kinds of wonders and many stories were told about his miracles.

There were, however, large groups of Jews who opposed the Hasidim. They clung to the old beliefs and thought that the noisy prayers and enthusiastic movements and gestures of the Hasidim were undignified and rowdy.

Rabbi Israel laughs

One Friday night the Baal Shem and his disciples were welcoming in the sacred day of rest, singing the Sabbath psalms, the Kabbalat Shabbat. As soon as the prayers had been recited, the rabbi sat in his chair, threw back his head and gave a great shout of laughter.

His disciples were quite taken aback, for they had never before seen their rabbi behave in such a strange way. They looked carefully at each other, and then around the room but they could not see anything which might have caused such hilarity.

The mystery deepened when, for a second time, the men saw the rabbi's shoulders shake and then his whole body heave with unrestrained merriment. They were far too respectful to ask their learned rabbi why he was so happy. Nevertheless when, once again, the Baal Shem burst out laughing until the tears rolled down his cheeks, Rabbi Kitzes, the most senior of the disciples, decided that something very unusual must have happened to amuse him so much. The moment the Sabbath ended he made up his mind to find out what it was.

The following day after the Havdalah ceremony—the hymns and prayers which bid farewell to the Sabbath day and separate it from the rest of the week—the rabbi sat in his study and lit his pipe. Rabbi Kitzes was, as always, invited in to discuss all kinds of rabbinical matters. On this occasion, however, he could hardly wait to ask a question of a different kind!

'Please tell us, rabbi, why you laughed so heartily on three separate occasions yesterday?' he asked.

'Have patience, my dear rabbi, and you will soon find out,' he replied.

As soon as the Sabbath had ended it was the Baal Shem's custom to take a ride into the countryside. On this occasion he ordered his carriage and invited only his closest disciples to accompany him.

The coachman drove on and on through the night and the Baal Shem told no one of their destination. It was only at daybreak, when the carriage stopped outside the house of the head of the Jewish community, that they recognized the little town of Kozenitz.

Good news travels fast, and in next to no time the whole town was talking of nothing else but the honour bestowed on them by the Baal Shem's visit. Many of his followers came to stand at a respectful distance just for a glimpse of his holy, radiant face. After the morning prayers had been recited, the Baal Shem asked the head of the community if he would be kind enough to send for Reb Shabsi the bookbinder. 'Shabsi, the bookbinder?' the elder repeated in surprise. 'With respect, rabbi, why do you want to see him? He may well be a skilled craftsman, but when all is said and done he is not very learned in the ways of the Torah.' And, standing on his dignity, he continued: 'Although Kozenitz is only a small town, it can supply you with many eminent scholars with whom you would surely have more in common than Shabsi.'

The Baal Shem ignored the elder's protests. 'I need to speak to Reb Shabsi on an urgent matter,' he insisted. Reluctantly, the elder agreed and sent a special messenger to summon Reb Shabsi, and his wife, Leah.

When they arrived the rabbi greeted them both warmly and offered them a seat. Then he spoke to the bookbinder: 'Shabsi, I want you to tell everyone here exactly what happened on Friday. Take your time, do not leave anything out and above all tell the truth.'

Shabsi was modest and shy, but, encouraged by the rabbi, he began: 'My dear rabbi, I am an honest man and have nothing to hide. If I have sinned in any way, I trust I will be punished accordingly. As you know I am a skilled bookbinder. It is not a lucrative trade, but when my order book is full I make quite a good living. Every Thursday I give Leah enough money to buy what we need for the Sabbath *challahs* (the traditional plaited Sabbath loaf), fish, meat, wine for the Sabbath benediction and candles to light in honour of the Sabbath. Every Friday I close my shop at ten o'clock and go to the synagogue. I pray there all day until the end of the evening service. That is my weekly routine and I keep to it as regularly as clockwork.

'It is only natural that the advancing years have taken their toll. My eyesight is poor and I no longer have the stamina to work long hours. As a result my income has dropped and we live from hand to mouth. There are times when I dread Thursday, especially when I have not earned enough money to give Leah for the Sabbath purchases. But my Friday habits never change—come what may I lock up my shop at ten o'clock and go straight to the synagogue.

'Last week I had no money—not a single groschen—to give Leah, nor did I know anyone from whom I could borrow, not even the price of a challah. I cannot bring myself to ask anyone for money, I am too proud to beg. You see, I place my trust entirely in God's hands and if He has failed to provide me with the essentials for the Sabbath it is not for me to question Him.

'On Friday I told my wife that I would return home much later than usual. I had planned to wait until everyone had left the synagogue. If I walked back past my house with them, I knew they would ask why there were no Sabbath candles burning.

'I was also concerned about Leah. I know that if she so much as hinted about our situation to the neighbours, they would give her challah and other food. I made her promise that on no account should she tell anyone nor accept charity.

'It was quite late when I returned from the synagogue, and I was astonished to see candles burning. I naturally thought that my wife had ignored my warning, and poured out our troubles to the neighbours. But that wasn't all. The table had been set with challahs and wine for the Sabbath blessing. My wife, bless her, is a good cook and in spite of myself I could not ignore the wonderful smell of *tzimmes*—beef and carrot stew! Just the same I asked no questions because it is a sin to break the peace of the Sabbath.

'But Leah knew at once that I was annoyed, and as soon as I had recited the Sabbath blessing, she explained what had happened. As soon as I had left that morning, Leah had started to clean and tidy the house in readiness for the Sabbath. Then she sorted the contents of an old clothes chest—a task she had put off for a long time. To her surprise she found an old jacket which she had mislaid and forgotten about. You can imagine her excitement when she saw that the buttons were made of silver!'

Shabsi smiled at the rabbi and went on: 'My wife sold the buttons and used the money to buy candles, challahs, wine, fish and meat, and after all that there was even some money left!

'There were tears of joy in my eyes when I heard this news, and I thanked the Heavenly Father again and again, It was such a relief to know that we could keep the Sabbath day in a decent way without anybody else's help.

'And because I was so happy, I did the first thing that came into my head. I stood up, took Leah's hand and we danced round the table. Then we sat down to get our breath, looked at each other and burst out laughing. After we had drunk our soup, we stood up and danced round the table again. This time we nearly split our sides we were laughing so much. And so it went on; after we had eaten the tzimmes we got up and danced again, quite helpless with merriment. What a time we had!

'That is my story, Holy Rabbi, and it is for you to judge if you think I have sinned. But God knows, my behaviour was not meant to be disrespectful in any way, it was purely spontaneous—to praise and thank Him for His grace and loving kindness.'

When Shabsi had finished speaking, the Baal Shem spoke to the elders and his disciples. 'When Reb Shabsi and his wife laughed and danced for joy, it had an immediate effect on the angels in heaven. They joined in and the ripples of their laughter echoed through the celestial halls. And if they could not restrain themselves, how could I? So I joined in too, and laughed three times.'

Then the Baal Shem put his hand on Shabsi's shoulder and asked, 'Tell me what you desire more than anything else. Would you like to be rich and live in luxury, or would you rather have a son to comfort you in your old age?' 'With respect, Rabbi, we have never set great store on wealth for its own sake. We are getting on in years and to our regret we have not been blessed with children. A child would bring its own rich reward,' Shabsi replied.
'Go in peace, then,' said the Baal Shem, 'and before the year is over Leah will bear you a son. I will come to the circumcision and act as his godfather myself. Perhaps you could name him Israel after me?'

And everything happened just as Rabbi Israel had prophesied. Reb Shabsi, the bookbinder, and his wife Leah were blessed with a baby son whom they called Israel. The Baal Shem was the honoured guest at the circumcision celebration, acted as the child's godfather and gave him his blessing. And when the child grew up he himself became a learned preacher and famous for his great wisdom.

King David's scroll

According to legend the one hundred and fifty psalms in the Bible's Book of Psalms were written by King David himself. The psalms themselves were preserved by scribes but no one knows what happened to King David's original writing, which has not been seen since the destruction of the Temple in Jerusalem. According to the legend, whoever finds the original Book of Psalms, written on a scroll in David's own hand, and returns it to the Holy Land will witness the return of the Messiah. Then the 'End of Days' will begin, and everyone will receive his just reward.

Israel ben Eliezer, the Baal Shem Tov, was one of those who firmly believed that King David's Book of Psalms still existed. He vowed that he would find the scroll and bring it to the Holy Land, for he longed for the coming of the Messiah more than anything else.

But the question of where he might begin the search was a constant source of worry. He realized that the answer could only be learned from heaven and, since he wished so fervently for the Messiah, one night his soul flew upwards, to the very Throne of Glory. There it pleaded to be told where the scroll was hidden and, among the angels' songs of praise, his soul heard the echoes of a celestial voice proclaiming that it was to be found in Constantinople in the library of the Sultan of Turkey.

The soul returned with the news to the body of the Baal Shem who decided there and then to set out on the long journey from his home in Poland. A sea voyage in those far-off days was long and hazardous. The Baal Shem left his home after Rosh Hashanah, the Jewish New Year, and only reached Constantinople at Passover time, more than six months later.

As soon as he disembarked, the Baal Shem went to the cemetery. There he prayed by the grave of Rav Naftali, a pious man who, many years earlier, had attempted to sail to the Holy Land but had died on the way. Rav Naftali's grave had become a kind of shrine where Jewish travellers, on their way to the Holy Land, would stop and pray. That night Rav Naftali appeared to the Baal Shem in a dream. He told him that Heaven had decreed that he might fulfil the task of restoring King David's Book of Psalms to the Jewish people. Alas, it would not be possible for the Baal Shem to return it to the Holy Land, for the time had not yet come for the Messiah to herald the End of Days.

The next morning the Baal Shem remembered his dream in every detail. He was overjoyed that Heaven had sanctioned his quest for the Book of Psalms, and yet saddened to know that he would never see the Messiah. Nevertheless he understood full well that each man has his own destiny to fulfil, whatever it may be.

The next day he walked about the streets of Constantinople trying to think of a credible reason for presenting himself to the sultan. He could not help noticing that wherever he went the people looked sad and dejected as if they were in a state of mourning. Curiosity got the better of him and he stopped a passer-by. 'Why is everyone so filled with gloom?' he asked.

The man heaved a deep sigh. 'Our beloved princess is ill and so far the most eminent physicians have not found a cure,' he said. 'The sultan has offered a reward of half his kingdom to anyone who is able to restore her to health.' Then the man looked grave and added: 'But whoever tries and fails will be put to death.'

The Baal Shem knew at once that this was none other than a sign from Heaven. Provided that he was able to cure the princess—and he had only one chance to do so—he would be in a position to request the Book of Psalms from the sultan himself. Once again he returned to Rav Naftali's grave and prayed fervently that he might learn the secret remedy.

His prayers were answered. As soon as he fell asleep he dreamed he saw Rav Naftali who told him that the princess's life could be saved by a rare species of delicate flower which flourished in the dark. It grew in a cave near the top of a mountain overlooking the city.

When he awoke, the Baal Shem again recalled every part of his dream. As soon as he had made the necessary preparations he set off to find the cave.

It did not take him long to reach the mountain and make his way up its steep slopes to the mouth of the cave. He stooped at the entrance to kindle a torch, and held it up to light the way ahead. He had not gone very far when he saw a most extraordinary sight. Through the flickering torchlight he saw a small patch of the most beautiful, fragrant pale white flowers, each one more exquisitely formed than the next. The Baal Shem bent down, gently picked one of the fragile blooms and carried it carefully back to Constantinople.

As soon as he reached the palace the Baal Shem announced that he had found a cure for the sick princess. He was granted an audience with the sultan who was both shocked and surprised to see a poorly dressed Jew enter the state room.

The Baal Shem bowed low. 'If Your Majesty will describe the princess's symptoms, I will try to cure her,' he said.

The sultan who was desperate to save his daughter's life, replied immediately, 'My daughter is obsessed by a dream. Night after night she sees the same white flower. She has drawn it for us many times but our learned botanists have told her that it cannot be found. Yet she continues to pine away for a flower that only exists in her dream.'

To the amazement and delight of the sultan, the Baal Shem showed him the wonderful pale flower which he had found in the cave. There was no doubt that it was exactly the same as the one in the princess's drawings. The sultan and the Baal Shem went immediately to the princess's room.

When she saw the precious bloom she burst into tears and sobbed: 'That is my flower—that is the one that I have dreamed about every night, the flower that no one else could find.'

The sultan soothed the princess and when she was calm, she looked at the flower again and realized that her dream had come true at last. From that moment, the princess's health was quickly restored to normal.

The sultan was overjoyed to see his daughter looking so much better. He was full of gratitude to the Baal Shem and, honouring his agreement, he offered him half his kingdom. To his complete astonishment the Baal Shem refused, asking instead for permission to look through the books in the sultan's library and to select one of them. The sultan agreed at once.

The sultan's library contained the largest and most important collection of books and manuscripts in Turkey and the Baal Shem was shown into a series of immense rooms each one lined from floor to ceiling with shelves. His heart sank when he realized the enormity of his task. But the divine spirit guided him to the cherished scroll he had been seeking for so long. And when he opened it and saw the words that King David himself had written hundreds of years before, songs of praise which he knew so well by heart, he was overwhelmed with joy.

The Baal Shem thanked the sultan and went to Rav Naftali's tomb for the third time. He placed the Book of Psalms on the grave so that the soul of the sage could share in its great blessing. And later that night the Baal Shem had a third dream.

On this occasion Rav Naftali told him that he had performed a remarkable mitzvah in restoring the precious scroll to the Jewish people. But now the scroll must be carefully hidden away again until the time was right for it to be taken to the Holy Land. As Rav Naftali had warned him in his first dream, the Baal Shem could not go there. Instead he should take the scroll back to Poland and place it in a secret mountain cave near the city of Kamenetz. The sage told him the holy words which he would need to open the entrance to the cave and once the Book was safely inside, to seal it up again.

The next morning the Baal Shem remembered everything in his dream and carefully carried out all the holy sage's instructions. King David's Book of Psalms is still hidden in that mountain cave awaiting the time when the footsteps of the Messiah are heard throughout the land. Then the one whose destiny it is to break the seal will carry King David's Book of Psalms to the Holy Land and the days of the Messiah will finally be at hand.

How high—that high?

The New Year festival is the time when Jewish people ask God's forgiveness for their sins of the past year and prepare for Yom Kippur—the Day of Atonement, which is the most solemn day in the Jewish calendar. It is marked by prayer and fasting from sunset to sunset. The ten-day period between the two festivals is known as the time of Selichot, or penitential prayers.

There was once a devout widow who regularly attended the evening Selichot services to prepare herself spiritually for Yom Kippur. Unlike the rest of the year, when worshippers attended synagogue for services in the morning, afternoon and evening, the Selichot prayers were held well after midnight. It was the duty of the shammes, the synagogue attendant, to go round the little town knocking on doors and windows to announce the time and remind members of the community that the service would shortly begin.

The widow thought it would be too shameful to fall asleep and miss the shammes's signal, so she decided not to go to bed, but to sit up, stay awake and listen out for him. Despite her good resolutions, her eyes grew heavy and very soon she was fast asleep in her chair.

A loud knocking woke her up with a start. 'Wake up, everyone, and come to synagogue for Selichot!' boomed the shammes's familiar voice. Relieved that she had heard his call in good time, the widow wrapped a shawl around her shoulders and stepped out into the dark street.

She had just locked her door, when a man passed by her house. He called out from the shadows: 'Are you going to synagogue for Selichot?'
'Indeed I am,' she answered.
'Then let us go together,' the stranger said.

Truth to tell, the widow was afraid of walking alone at night and welcomed the offer of an escort. Not another soul could be seen. It was as if the whole town was fast asleep and the only sound that could be heard was the echo of their footsteps.
'I wonder where everyone is?' the widow asked nervously. 'Surely they were woken by the shammes's call just as I was?'
'Of course they were, but we were probably a bit slow getting started. By the time we get to synagogue, everyone will already be in their seats,' the stranger reassured her.

But when they arrived, all they could see was the flickering lamp of the Ner Tamid—the eternal light—suspended before The Ark of the Torah, making the shadows dance round the dark, deserted building. The stranger remained in the main body of the synagogue, while the widow, clutching her prayer book, went upstairs to her seat in the women's gallery. She sat there alone, frightened and waiting, waiting—but no one came.

Curious to see what the stranger was doing, the widow looked down at the exact moment he looked up at her. His dark, flashing eyes held her spellbound in his gaze. In spite of all her efforts she could not tear her eyes away—it was as if she was held in a dreadful trance.

Suddenly the stranger stretched his hand towards her, and she watched in horror, as it grew longer and longer, its bony fingers bent like claws, until it reached right into the women's gallery. The fingers were just about to

clutch her throat, when in desperation she began to recite the most sacred prayer at the top of her voice. 'Shema Yisrael Adonai Elohenu, Adonai Echad! Hear, O Israel, the Lord our God, the Lord is One.'

The very act of prayer seemed to release her paralysed body. She tore the clutching fingers from her neck, ran down the stairs and out into the street. She did not stop until she was certain that no one was following her.

Panting for breath she prayed fervently, 'Almighty God, thank you for saving me from the devil,' for she realized, with a shudder, that the stranger was no other than a demon in disguise.

As soon as the widow arrived home, she heard the chimes of midnight from the town clock—it was still much too early for the shammes to start his rounds. Once again she settled herself comfortably in a chair to await his knock. Overcome with exhaustion, she was soon snoring away in a sound sleep.

'Children of Israel, come and repent!' shouted the shammes as he banged on her door. The widow woke with a start, and wearing her warm shawl well tucked round her, she once again locked up her house and stepped out into the street.

To her great relief, she was joined by a crowd of worshippers, yawning, rubbing sleep from their tired eyes and all streaming along in the same direction. It was a comforting sight to see the lights of the synagogue in the distance.

As she pattered along, deep in thought, a Jew, holding a large prayer book in his hand, caught up with her. 'Do you mind if we walk together to the synagogue?' he asked politely.

'Not at all,' the widow replied kindly, grateful for a companion on such a dark night. 'Do you know,' the widow went on, 'I am just beginning to recover from the most terrible shock.'

'Really?' replied the man. 'Whatever happened?'

The widow poured out her troubles. 'I had just dozed off to sleep when I was woken by the call for Selichot. Just outside my door I saw a Jew who offered to accompany me to the synagogue. I saw no harm in that, after all, he looked no different from yourself or any other pious Jew for that matter. He had a black beard and carried a large prayer book, just like yours. As we were the first to arrive at the synagogue, I went up to the women's gallery to wait for the others, and the man remained below. I cannot really describe what happened next. All I know is that I seemed to be hypnotized by his powerful gaze, and slowly but surely he reached out his hand towards me, and it grew longer and longer.'

'How far did it stretch?' asked the man, fascinated by the widow's account.

'May God punish me if this is not the exact truth, but I swear his hand reached right up to the women's gallery!' she gasped.

The man was astonished. 'May the Lord preserve us! How high do you think his hand stretched?' he asked.

'It is hard to say exactly, but I think it was so high,' and the widow stood on tiptoe and pointed her arm straight up above her.

'Do you mean like this?' the man asked her, raising his own arm which began to grow longer and longer until it reached the top of a tall tree.

The expression on the poor widow's face was one of disbelief, which quickly changed to one of terror. She opened her mouth to scream but no sound came out. So she mouthed the words of the prayer: 'Hear, O Israel, the Lord our God, the Lord is One.' Then she fled.

She did not dare to look behind, nor could she block out the sound of loud, harsh, mocking laughter which followed her until she arrived breathless at the gates of the synagogue. Trembling in every limb, she once more climbed the stairs to the women's gallery. 'What has happened to me tonight is a warning from Heaven.' she thought. And not only on that night, but for the entire ten days of Selichot, the widow remained wide awake waiting for the shammes's call to synagogue, where she prayed earnestly to God to forgive her sins.

Tales of the festivals

The Hebrew calendar is a lunar calendar and records not only the dates of the festivals and fast days which are an integral part of Jewish life, but also the dates of the new moon when special prayers are recited in synagogue. All these festivals recall and honour special events of national, religious or historical significance.

There are three pilgrim festivals, two High festivals and six minor festivals, of which Hanukkah and Purim are more widely celebrated than the rest.

In the Book of Exodus, God commands, 'Three times a year you shall keep a pilgrim-feast to me' and the three pilgrim festivals are joyful occasions: the festivals of Pesach (Passover), Pentecost or Shavuot (the Feast of Weeks) and Sukkoth (Tabernacles). These are known as the *shalosh regalim* and commemorate the times when the Jews made special pilgrimages to Jerusalem to make sacrifices and to bring offerings of the choicest first fruits to the Temple.

These religious festivals coincided with agricultural seasons. Thus Passover celebrates the Exodus from Egypt, and the barley crop is sown at that time. Shavuot, seven weeks later, falls at the time when the barley crop is ripe and it also commemorates the giving of the Torah to the Children of Israel. Sukkoth is the harvest festival and also describes the time the Children of Israel spent in the Wilderness on their way to the Promised Land. Sukkoth or booths are built and decorated with fruits, as a reminder of the temporary dwellings the Israelites used in the Wilderness.

The High Holy Days—Rosh Hashanah (the Jewish New Year) and Yom Kippur (the Day of Atonement) differ from the other festivals in that they are more concerned with the individual. The New Year is the time for a fresh start when a person examines his past life and prepares himself spiritually for the most solemn day in the Hebrew calendar, Yom Kippur, the Day of Atonement. Jews spend this day in synagogue in prayer and fasting, asking God's forgiveness for past sins.

The festivals of Purim and Hanukkah, whose origins are told here, are, without doubt, those that remain the most popular with Jewish children, and the ones they can celebrate in the most festive way.

113

Queen Esther
and the Festival of Purim

According to the Book of Esther in the Bible, the Festival of Purim is celebrated every year on the fourteenth day of the Hebrew month of Adar to commemorate the deliverance of the Jews of Persia from the wicked Haman, who had plotted their death in the middle of the fifth century before the Common Era.

The festival is called Purim from the Hebrew word *purim* which means 'lots'. In ancient times it was common practice to cast lots by tossing coloured or specially marked stones onto the ground. Decisions were reached from the pattern made by the stones when they fell. Purim refers to the lots cast by Haman to determine the day on which he planned the destruction of the Jews of Persia.

In honour of Purim a special service is held in the synagogue. The Book of Esther is read aloud in Hebrew from a Megillah or scroll. Long before books were printed scribes wrote on pieces of parchment which would then be stitched together and rolled up to form a scroll. Everyone listens carefully and as soon as Haman's name is mentioned they stamp their feet, or hiss and boo. To add to the noise 'greggers', a kind of grinding rattle, are shaken. This is done to fulfil the command: 'May his name be blotted out.'

Purim is a happy festival full of celebrations in honour of brave Queen Esther. A Purim Shpiel or play is traditionally performed at this time as a means of retelling the Purim story. There are fancy dress parades and parties, money is collected for the poor, and gifts of cakes, biscuits and sweets are sent to families and friends. This is an old custom called *misloach manot* which means 'sending gifts'. Delicious poppy-seed cakes called *hamantoshen*—Haman's pockets—are eaten only at Purim time.

King Ahasuerus, of Shushan in Persia, made no secret of his wealth and power. He entertained foreign dignitaries, provincial governors and members of his court on a lavish scale. On one such occasion he gave a banquet in the gardens of the royal pavilion to which he invited not only important visitors, but all the people of Shushan. There was an abundance of the finest food, wine flowed freely and everyone was in a happy mood. Meanwhile, as was the custom of the times, Queen Vashti entertained the wives in a separate part of the palace. In those days women were confined to their own quarters out of reach of the prying eyes of strange men. Having drunk too much wine, the king began to boast openly about his wife.

'The queen is the most beautiful woman in all Persia,' he bragged. 'What is more I will prove it. Send for the queen,' he ordered. The guests waited for the queen to appear and started to whisper among themselves when the royal messenger returned alone.

The king was incensed. Not only had he been publicly embarrassed, but Vashti had flouted Persian law by disobeying her husband and, more seriously, a royal command. Vashti was banished from the court as an example to other wayward wives. As soon as she was gone, plans were made to select a new queen.

The women's quarters of the royal palace were soon filled with a stream of young and beautiful women waiting to be presented to the king. Among them was a striking young Jewish woman called Esther.

When Esther's parents died she had come to live with her Uncle Mordecai who was a scribe in the palace. In those days very few people could read and write and for a fee a scribe would compile letters and documents for his clients. Mordecai warned Esther: 'Remember, while you are at court, do not tell anyone that you are a Jew. There are those who would do us great harm,' he said.

Many young girls were brought before King Ahasuerus, but his heart went out to Esther, not only for her beauty but for her gentleness and charm. He placed a crown on her head and made her his queen.

Mordecai worked in the palace courtyard which was at the centre of the royal household. One day he overheard two guards plotting to murder the king. Mordecai quickly sent a message to Esther, who warned her husband.

The plot was duly discovered and the guilty men hanged. This event was written down in the royal chronicles.

About this time King Ahasuerus promoted Haman, a court official, to the rank of chief adviser. Already well known for his cruelty and conceit, Haman soon took advantage of his new position of authority by ordering everyone to bow down before him. Everyone obeyed, everyone, that is, except Mordecai.

Haman was beside himself with fury. 'How dare you stand, when all must bow down before me. Who are you to disobey me?' he demanded.
'I am Mordecai the Jew. My people do not bow down to men as if to worship them. We pray only to Almighty God,' Mordecai answered with quiet dignity.

Haman had heard enough to convince himself that he must take revenge. He hated Mordecai because he was a Jew and had defied him. He planned to get rid of him and all the Jews in Persia but he required the king's permission to carry out his vile scheme.

As soon as he was granted an audience with the king, Haman broached the matter uppermost in his mind. 'There are a people in your kingdom who are different from us. They follow their own strange laws and disobey the rules of the land,' he lied. 'They are a menace and a danger to you and with your permission I will deal with them.'

The king was apt to take Haman's advice on important matters of state. 'Do as you see fit,' he said and gave Haman his ring. The ring was embossed with the royal seal and was used to represent the king's signature.

Haman lost no time in casting lots to find a suitable date. Then he issued a decree which stated that on the thirteenth day of the Hebrew month of Adar all Jews would be killed and their possessions confiscated. The document bore the king's seal and a copy was sent to every province in Persia.

When the Jewish people heard the dreadful news, they reacted first with disbelief and then with terror. They tore their clothes and put ashes on their heads as a sign of grief and mourning. The queen shuddered with horror

when she read the decree and sent for Mordecai. 'You must go to the king and beg him to spare our people,' he advised her. The queen went pale. 'You know I can only see the king if he sends for me. If I go to his inner court unannounced I may be put to death,' she faltered.
'It is the only way to save us,' Mordecai whispered sadly.
'You are right,' Esther replied firmly. 'I cannot watch helplessly while that vicious man destroys us. I would rather disobey the king and die than let my people perish. I will fast for

three days before I go and see him. Ask the Jews to pray for me,' she added gently.

The queen fasted and prayed and considered how she might foil Haman's plot. Then, dressed in her finest clothes, she summoned her courage and walked to the entrance of the king's inner courtroom.

When Ahasuerus saw her he stretched out his sceptre as a sign that he would receive her. The queen's face shone with relief and joy as she entered.

'Why did you risk your life to see me?' he asked. 'What is it you want? Only tell me and I will gladly share half of my kingdom with you.'

The queen was filled with hope by these words, but decided to keep the real reason to herself. She thanked the king. 'Your Majesty, it would give me great pleasure if you and your chief minister would attend a banquet which I have prepared in your honour,' she said.

Haman was flattered by an invitation of such distinction and joined the king in the queen's apartments where the two guests were treated with great hospitality. Later Ahasuerus again asked Esther to make her request but she was still not ready to reveal her true intentions. 'If Your Majesty and Haman will favour me with your presence here tomorrow I will speak of the matter then,' she said.

Within the privacy of his home, Haman confided to his wife: 'I must be held in high esteem by both the king and queen to be welcomed to a second banquet. But my position is continually undermined by that stubborn Jew, Mordecai. I wish him dead,' he rasped. 'Listen,' his wife suggested, 'in the morning go and ask the king for permission to hang Mordecai and at the same time you can order a gallows to be made for him.'

Haman went to bed to dream of his villainous plan. Meanwhile at the palace, the king was unable to sleep. To while away the time he followed the affairs of state recorded in the royal chronicles. He read how Mordecai the Jew had uncovered a plot to murder him. But there was no mention of Mordecai having received any reward for saving his life. 'Send for Haman,' ordered the king.

Haman hurried to the palace. It must be a good omen to be summoned to the palace at such an early hour, he thought.

'How can I best show my gratitude to a man who has loyally served his king?' Ahasuerus asked him. Haman felt sure that the king meant himself, so he gushed, 'Dress him in royal robes, place a crown on his head, and set him on the king's horse. Then appoint a nobleman to lead him through the city calling out, "Here is the man the king wishes to honour"'. The king readily accepted these suggestions and to Haman's utter consternation, he was ordered to bestow all the honours on Mordecai!

Haman's pride suffered a severe blow. Not only was his plan to hang Mordecai hastily postponed, but he was forced to watch the crowds cheering Mordecai as he led his horse through the streets of Shushan.

That evening Haman and the king attended the queen's second banquet. When they had finished eating and drinking Esther spoke quietly: 'Your Majesty, a decree has been passed in your name stating that all the Jews of Persia are to be killed. I, too, am a Jew and must die with my people.'

The king was shocked. 'Who gave this order?' he shouted.

'This evil man,' answered Esther, pointing at Haman. Then she threw herself at the king's feet.

'I have only one request. I beg of you, withdraw this terrible edict and let me and my people live,' she pleaded.

From that moment events happened quickly. Haman was seized and sent to the gallows which he had prepared for Mordecai. The king sent for Mordecai, appointed him chief minister in Haman's place and gave him his ring.

The king spoke to Mordecai and Esther. 'Not even a king can change a royal decree,' he said, 'but I can grant your request in a different way. A law will be passed stating that the Jews can take up arms against their enemies. Mordecai can use my ring and send copies to every province in the country.'

The new chief adviser lost no time in carrying out the king's instructions. Mordecai's reputation as a man the king trusted spread far and wide. The Jews of Persia were proud of him and gained confidence. And on the thirteenth day of Adar the dreadful decree was averted—the Jews defended themselves well and triumphed over their attackers.

Then Esther and Mordecai sent a message to all the Jews of Persia asking them to keep the fourteenth day of Adar as a special day of celebration. When the Jews heard how Queen Esther had saved their lives there was great feasting and rejoicing. People sent each other gifts of food and money was collected for the poor. From that day nearly 2,500 years ago to this, Jews all over the world have celebrated the festival of Purim every year.

Hanukkah, the festival of lights

The festival of Hanukkah begins on the twenty-fifth day of the Hebrew month of Kislev (which roughly corresponds to December) and lasts for eight days. Hanukkah commemorates two important events. Judah Maccabee, a member of the priestly family of Hasmoneans, and his small volunteer army triumphed over the brutal and powerful Syrian Greek ruler, Antiochus IV, in 175 BCE. In Hebrew, *hanukkah* means 'dedication' and the festival also celebrates the re-dedication of the Temple which had been desecrated by Antiochus.

The events connected with the festival of Hanukkah are related in the First and Second Books of Maccabees. These books were not considered sacred, and therefore were not included in the Hebrew Bible. Nevertheless they provide an important source of information about the Holy Land during the second century before the Common Era.

Although the meaning of the word *maccabee* is uncertain it is usually translated as 'hammer' no doubt referring to Judah's great strength. The word in Hebrew is also an acrostic of the first letter of the Hebrew words *Mi Kamocha Baelim Adonai* which means 'Who among the mighty is like You, O God?' It may well have served as a rallying cry for the Jews in their battle against Antiochus.

During the eight days of Hanukkah, known also as the Festival of Lights, a blessing is recited and candles are lit and placed in a special nine-branched candelabrum called a menorah or hannukia. On the first night a candle called a shammes or attendant is lit and is used to light all the others—one additional candle on each consecutive night of the festival. The lighted candles commemorate the Miracle of the Cruse of Oil, which followed Judah's victory.

The festival of Hanukkah is especially attractive for children. There are many stirring songs and hymns which describe the Maccabean victories. Parties are held and children receive gifts of Hanukkah *gelt*, a Yiddish word for money. A popular game is played with a *dreidel* or *sevivon*—a small four-sided spinning top. Each side bears a Hebrew letter which together stand for the words 'A Great Miracle Happened There.' Delicious fried potato pancakes called *latkes* are eaten as well as doughnuts or *sufganiyot*. Both these dishes use oil which is symbolic of the Miracle of Hanukkah.

Like his father before him, Antiochus, the ruler of the Syrian Greeks, was motivated by ambition, power and greed. The more he had the more he wanted. He even built a huge city, Antioch, and called himself Epiphanes, which is Greek for 'The Manifest God'.
'I too will conquer the world like the great Alexander of Macedon,' he boasted.

Territorial gains were never enough; Antiochus wanted to strengthen his kingdom by imposing his own religion throughout the lands under his rule. So he crushed local customs and traditions and gained complete control by forcing his new subjects to worship Greek gods.

Not content with his previous victories, Antiochus chose Jerusalem for his next target. He called a meeting of his generals and told them: 'I have decided to conquer the Jews who live in the land of Israel. They are a strange people. They do not observe our laws, nor do they sacrifice to our gods—in fact they mock them. Not only will I fight and defeat them but I will destroy their religion and they will be forced to accept ours under penalty of death.'

Antiochus then equipped and dispatched a great army to the Holy Land. The walls of Jerusalem were breached, and the Temple

broken into and robbed of its treasures. Houses were looted and burned, Jews were killed indiscriminately and their women and children sold into slavery. Those who could, escaped to Alexandria, Babylonia, Persia and many other foreign countries. And throughout this period of terror there was no opposition, no one to organize any retaliation—the Jewish leaders remained silent and subdued.

The Jews called Antiochus 'The Madman'— with good reason. For any other conqueror, Jerusalem would have been the jewel in the crown. But there was no satisfying this cruel and brutal king—he was determined to crush the Jews completely by taking away their religion.

'Destroy the scrolls of the Torah and the Jewish academies of learning,' Antiochus ordered. Then he continued: 'Jews may no longer observe their dietary laws and circumcision of their male infants is forbidden. They are not allowed to keep their Sabbath day, instead they must bow down to our gods. Anyone seen practising Jewish customs will be put to death.' And Antiochus appointed his chief officers to undertake the persecution of the Jews.

The king's representatives did a thorough job. They travelled the length and breadth of the country ransacking synagogues and houses of study, and killing any Jews who opposed them. Meanwhile in Jerusalem, Antiochus's heathen priests placed a great statue of the god Zeus on the Temple altar, sacrificed a pig and sprinkled its unclean blood in the sanctuary. To the Jews this was the most abhorrent insult of all. Fearing for their lives, many of them fled, leaving the city desecrated and deserted.

In the village of Modein, not far from Jerusalem, there lived a highly respected Jew called Mattathias, an old priest of the Hasmonean clan. He had five sons, Yohanan, Simon, Judah, Eleazar and Jonathan.

About this time, a company of officers led by Apelles arrived at Modein, intent on forcing its inhabitants to sacrifice to their Greek gods. An altar was made ready and Mattathias, as one of the leaders of the village, was ordered to prepare the sacrificial offerings.

This was the last straw. Mattathias was a pious, God-fearing man and he was shocked and sickened by the reports of the abominable crimes Antiochus had committed in Jerusalem. He knew his life would be in danger if he refused Apelles' commands.

'I am an old man and have not long to live,' he said to himself. 'But of one thing I am certain. I will continue to uphold the tenets of the Jewish faith with my last breath. I will never worship false gods.' And he spoke angrily to his sons and the people of Modein: 'Listen to me, my brothers. Let the other nations who have been crushed by Antiochus worship Greek gods. But not us. We must rebel. Let us swear by the Almighty God that we shall never betray our faith.' And with these words he rushed up to Apelles, killed him with one blow and shouted: 'Take up arms. Whoever is for God and His Holy Law follow me!'

Mattathias and his sons escaped from the village with a small group of volunteers and hid in the Judean hills. From there, they embarked on a series of guerrilla attacks on the Greek units. What they lacked in numbers and weapons, they made up for in their religious zeal and a fierce hatred of the enemy. The Maccabean revolt had begun.

Mattathias led the rebellion for one year and just before he died he appointed his third son, Judah, to succeed him. In the short time since the formation of the Maccabees, Judah's strength, military talent and heroic deeds had already become well known. The old man blessed Judah: 'Serve God with all your heart and soul and bring redemption to Israel,' he said.

Judah respected his father's words and became a great leader in the sacred struggle against Antiochus. He brought new hope and courage to the Jewish people, many of whom returned from exile to join him.

Because of the size and strength of the Greek army, Judah's strategy had first been one of ambush rather than direct confrontation. But with increased numbers to swell his own ranks, and morale running high, he used his outstanding tactical skill to win many military victories.

Antiochus decided to travel to Persia to raise

the large sum of money he needed to maintain his powerful army. Before he left he appointed three generals—Ptolemy, Nikanor and Gorgias—with orders to shatter the strength of Israel and wipe out the remaining Jews in Jerusalem. They assembled forty thousand infantry, seven thousand cavalry and reinforcements from Syria, then they prepared to invade Judea. Their tents were pitched in the plains near the city of Emmaus. Foreign merchants, encouraged by the sheer size of the military operation, arrived in the camp with silver and gold coins and a supply of chains, ready to buy the Jews for slaves.

Judah and his men rallied at Mizpah. They fasted all day and prayed to God for strength and guidance. In accordance with bibilical law Judah sent home those men who felt afraid, those who were newly-weds, and those who were planting vineyards. Then they marched to the south of Emmaus and camped there. Judah told them: 'Tomorrow you must be ready to fight the enemy who want to destroy us and our holy place. It is better to die fighting than see disaster strike our people. But God alone will judge.'

Leaving the main part of his army at Emmaus and marching by night, Gorgias took five thousand men and one thousand hand-picked cavalry in order to take the Jewish army unawares. But Judah had secret information of this plan and decided to attack the king's army while it was divided. When they struck camp, Judah purposely left their fires burning in order to deceive and confuse Gorgias.

The Maccabees marched through the night to the enemy's well-fortified camp where the Greek soldiers outnumbered them several times over. Nevertheless Judah took heart from his plan to mount a surprise attack. He gave his men a final exhortation: 'Do not be afraid of their great numbers and do not panic when they charge. Remember how our fathers were saved at the Red Sea, when Pharaoh pursued them. Let us call on heaven to have mercy on us.' Then Judah gave the signal and the trumpeters sounded the battle call.

Judah's strategy was successful. The Greek soldiers, having assumed that Gorgias had destroyed the Maccabees, started to panic when they found themselves attacked. Judah took advantage of their confusion and slew many and pursued the rest as far as Gezer and Ashdod and Yavneh. Then Judah warned his men that the battle was not yet over. 'Do not forget that Gorgias and his army are not far away. Make sure that you are ready for them.'

And sure enough they soon saw a detachment of Gorgias's army in the hills near by. When the enemy looked down and saw their camp in flames they realized that the rest of their army had been defeated. And the sight of Judah's army drawn up ready for battle confirmed it. They retreated and fled in terror to Philistia.

Judah knew this was not the time to celebrate military victories. He led his brothers and his army to Jerusalem to cleanse and rededicate the Temple.

Everything was in ruins, from the altar to the priests' quarters. There was much work to be done, and it would be all the more rewarding because it was for the House of God. Judah selected priests who were devoted to the study of the Torah, and he gave orders for the interior of the Temple to be completely restored and a new altar made. Then new sacred vessels were made as well as a menorah or candelabrum.

Then Judah rededicated the Temple and offered incense and burnt offerings upon the altar. But when they were about to kindle the light in the menorah they found that the Greeks had defiled all the oil except for one small sealed jar. In those days, before candles were used, lights were made from wicks soaked in oil and now there was only enough oil to keep the candelabrum lights burning for one day. Then a miracle happened. The lights continued to burn for eight days—the time required to prepare a supply of fresh pure oil.

In order to commemorate this joyful occasion, Judah Maccabee and his brothers decreed that each year, on the twenty-fifth day of Kislev, the Jewish people would celebrate Hanukkah for eight days. During this time they were to burn lights, adding a new light each night, and sing songs of praise, to celebrate the triumph of Israel in its struggle for religious freedom.

Tales of longing

Jewish tradition has many differing beliefs about the coming of the Messiah or the 'Anointed One' as he is known. It is thought that he will come when great misfortune engulfs the Jewish people, as the sea engulfs the shore at flood-tide. Another firmly held belief is that the Messiah, the Son of David, will come to that generation which repents of its evil ways and turns to the path of righteousness.

The great longing for the coming of the Messiah has been the golden dream of the Jewish people throughout the ages. The greater their suffering, the more desperate the people became to reach out to the supernatural—a kind of wishful thinking. Delving into the hidden wisdom of the Cabbala—Jewish mysticism—they hoped to bring an end to their exile from the Land of Israel and an end to their suffering. It therefore became the single-minded objective of the cabbalists, the majority of whom were men of selfless and pure intention, to hasten the coming of the Messiah to free the Jewish people. To this end they were ready to make every personal sacrifice, even to give up their lives.

The story is told in the Talmud of two sages, Rabbi Simeon and Rabbi Hai who were travelling together through the night. They watched enthralled as the dawn broke and the first fingers of light appeared above the horizon. Rabbi Simeon turned to his companion and said, 'This is the way the Messiah will come, slowly and gradually and bathed in radiance like the rising sun.'

Of all the great cabbalist legends, that of Joseph della Reyna is the most dramatic and has stirred the imagination and emotions of many generations of readers. The story of the Lost Princess was written by Rabbi Nachman of Bratzlav, one of the great Jewish teachers and mystics, who lived from 1770 to 1811. Rabbi Nachman was renowned for his talent as a great storyteller and he was one of the leading personalities in the Hasidic movement. Although the story reads like a fairytale quest, the followers of Rabbi Nachman interpreted it as the search for the secret of the Shekinah—the Divine Presence—in exile. The overcoming of many difficulties and obstacles during the long search and the final reunion of father and daughter suggests the ultimate redemption of the Jewish people by the Almighty, and the coming of the Messianic age.

Rabbi Joseph storms Heaven

The holy city of Jerusalem was so full of good and pious men who believed in God and loved the truth, that Rabbi Joseph della Reyna decided that it was high time to hasten the coming of the Messiah.

He was under no illusions that the task would be an easy one, but he remained hopeful that he would succeed where others had failed.

Among his disciples were five men who were pure in heart and intention. They were cabbalists who had delved deeply into the secret truths of the Zohar—a collection of mystical writings. Day and night they sat over their holy books examining the hidden wisdom of this world and the next.

One night as they sat studying, Rabbi Joseph announced: 'My friends. God has blessed us with wisdom and knowledge. We have mastered the Cabbala and discovered the innermost secrets of the Torah, and through their power we are capable of performing great wonders. It is our sacred duty to use these exceptional gifts to drive all evil from the world, to hasten the coming of the Messiah, and bring back the Holy Shekina from its long exile.'

Then he paused and looked kindly at his devoted disciples. 'I have come to this decision after long soul-searching for I know that we will, together, be able to accomplish something that will amaze both Earth and Heaven. I have made detailed plans and all I need now is your unstinting help.'

There was not even a whisper of dissent. 'Holy Rabbi! We know that Almighty God, blessed be His Name, is with you and we will gladly assist you,' they replied.
'Good. Let us now prepare for our holy task. We must first bathe, put on clean white garments, and cut ourselves off from worldly interests for three days and nights in order to fast and pray. We shall need ample provisions for our journey into the wilderness, for we cannot return until we have successfully carried out our mission.

The disciples acted at once. They were deeply affected by the holiness of their task and caught up in the rabbi's enthusiasm and strength of purpose.

On the third day they found Rabbi Joseph praying with such fervour and ecstacy that his face shone with radiance. The rabbi looked up and greeted the men tenderly. 'Thank you, my beloved disciples, for having carried out my instructions. Now you are truly worthy of helping me in my sacred work. God will help us reach our goal by the power of His Holy Name.'
'Amen', the disciples answered fervently, 'Let us go!' And Rabbi Joseph della Reyna and his five disciples started out on their holy quest.

They travelled northwards to Meron and spent three days praying at the grave of the famous mystic, Rabbi Simeon bar Yohai.

When Rabbi Joseph had ended his vigil he fell asleep and dreamed that Rabbi Simeon rebuked him sharply: 'It was very rash of you and your disciples to undertake such a terrifying task! Be warned—you will fail miserably and you will be beset by insuperable difficulties and dangers. What is more, you will not survive the attempt and your souls will be condemned to everlasting purgatory. But since you are resolute, listen to my advice. Be discreet in word and deed, so that those evil spirits who wish you harm may be rendered powerless.'
'But God knows that my intentions are of the purest,' Joseph protested to Rabbi Simeon. 'I have spoken to Him many times about that. My aim is not a selfish one, it is for the good of all Jews and all mankind. He alone will guide me on the way.'

Rabbi Simeon nodded wisely and gave him his blessing: 'May God help you and keep you safely, wherever you go.'

When he awoke he told the men about his dream, and Rabbi Simeon's warning.

Later that day they left Meron and travelled on towards Tiberias, until they reached a large, cool, peaceful forest. There they spent several days absorbed in their sacred books of learning and purifying their bodies in the Sea of Galilee. Each time they immersed themselves they repeated holy formulas and incantations. They fasted during the day and ate only bread and water in the evening.

Then Rabbi Joseph invoked the power of the Cabbala and called on the Prophet Elijah: 'O Elijah,' he implored. 'Come and teach me how I should behave so that I may carry out my holy undertaking.'

No sooner had he finished praying than Elijah appeared. 'Tell me what you want, my good Rabbi, and I will help if I can,' he promised.

'Holy prophet,' the rabbi replied, 'I do not ask for myself, but only for the glory of God, blessed be His Name. Show me how I can make holiness triumph over evil and so bring redemption to all mankind.'

Elijah the Prophet looked sad. 'You have taken upon yourself a task that no human being can possibly accomplish,' he told the rabbi. 'You must be as holy and pure as the angels themselves in order to triumph over Satan and his demons. Nevertheless your aim is an exalted one and, should you succeed, you will be the happiest man on Earth. However, I must tell you that you are attempting something beyond human strength. Take my advice—abandon your plan!'

And Rabbi Joseph wept. 'Dear Prophet of God,' he pleaded, 'how can I give up what I have started? Do not forsake me now for it is too late to turn back. I have sworn before God that I will not rest until I have driven Satan from the Earth, welcomed the Messiah, and restored the Shekina to the glory it had when the Temple still stood in Jerusalem. You know that I am willing to sacrifice my life—I beg you to guide me along the right path.'

Elijah, full of compassion, replied, 'Your tears have touched my heart. I will help you if I can.'

Then Elijah gave him careful and detailed instructions as to how he was to invoke the Angel Sandalfon by means of fasting, prayer, and cabbalistic formulas. 'And do not forget to recite the verse: Praise be His Name whose glorious kingdom is forever and ever!' Elijah reminded him. 'Only then can you ask the Angel Sandalfon what you should do to remove wickedness from the Earth. If you do as I say, and if the Almighty God wills it so, then you will be able to bring Redemption to all the

world.' And having blessed the rabbi and his disciples, the prophet vanished.

Everything happened just as Elijah had said. At the end of twenty-one days, amid a great tumult from Heaven, and with a pillar of flame before them, the Angel Sandalfon and his host of Seraphim swept down to Earth.

Trembling with fear, Rabbi Joseph and his disciples fell on their faces and recited the prayer just as Elijah had counselled. Then they dared to look up at the angels clothed in flame and splendour.

The Angel Sandalfon spoke to them in a voice like thunder: 'O, sinful mortals! Why have you caused so much turmoil throughout the Seven Heavens? How dare you call on us to descend to the sinful Earth. Stop this madness at once!'

Rabbi Joseph was too terrified to speak. But gradually he found the courage to reply. 'Holy Angel Sandalfon! I beg of you to believe that I meant no disrespect. I am working only for the glory of God and His Holy Torah. I could no longer bear to see my people being trampled underfoot by our enemies. My sincere aim is to bring the Messiah, and return the Shekina to its former glory. I beg of you, Holy Angel, to show me the right path!'

Sandalfon began to change his attitude. 'May God be with you until you reach your goal!' he announced. 'Rest assured that all the angels in Heaven feel for you. But I must warn you of difficulties ahead, for Satan and the demons have untold power which even we are unable to conquer. You can only achieve your aim if God Himself stands by you and believes that the time is right for the coming of the Messiah. And, should you fail, you may strengthen Satan's hand so that he will do even greater harm.'

Rabbi Joseph felt deserted. Even the mighty Sandalfon was not prepared to help! Then he called to his followers, who were lying prostrate with fear on the ground: 'Rise up and join with me in prayer—who knows, we may soften the angel's heart.'

And they prayed to God and pleaded with the angel again.

Sadly, Sandalfon replied: 'Alas I cannot help you, I have no power over Satan nor do I know how you can triumph over him and his demons. My sole duty is to make sure that the prayers of the righteous rise to Heaven and reach the Throne of God. However, if you are so determined you must speak to the Angel Metatron and his hosts. It is their task to prevent Satan from growing stronger. Metatron dwells in the Seventh Heaven next to the Heavenly Throne and appears as a pillar of fire more blinding than the sun's rays. Reflect on my words and stop before it is too late!'

But Rabbi Joseph would not listen, 'Forgive me but I cannot change my plans now. Please tell me, how can I bring the Angel Metatron to Earth?'

Sandalfon saw that nothing would make the rabbi abandon his quest, so he relented and gave him and his five assistants detailed instructions on how, through further fasting, prayer and purifying themselves in the Sea of Galilee, they would be ready to pronounce the Divine name of God and call upon Metatron, the guardian of this mystic name.
'Be strong in spirit,' he called out to them and then, still preceded by a pillar of fire, he returned with his angels to Heaven.

The heavenly hosts could talk of nothing else but Rabbi Joseph's obstinacy and his daring attempt to bring the Messiah to Earth. The Anointed One himself was confident that he would soon descend astride his white horse to deliver mankind from evil.

Yet while everyone above was hopeful, Satan sat gnashing his teeth in the depths of Gehenna below. He discussed the rumours with his wife, Lilith. Lilith was furious:
'Our very existence is threatened and yet you sit doing nothing. Go at once and complain to God.' And Satan obeyed her.
'The angels wish to make an end of me before my time has come,' Satan snapped. 'Tell me, O Lord, how can the Messiah come when there are so many sinners among the Jews? As for this misguided fool Joseph della Reyna, I would like your permission to get rid of him.'

But God refused, for He knew that through all their hardships, prayers, fasting and sacred thoughts, the band of pious men were well protected.

And when Satan continued to press his point God answered: 'I alone have the power to announce the Messiah's coming, and if the Jews possess a saint such as Joseph della Reyna they are indeed worthy to hasten his arrival.' But the Almighty had one last word: 'However, if he strays from righteousness by as much as a hair's breadth, I will give you the power to foil his plan.'

Meanwhile, Rabbi Joseph and his disciples again prepared to purify their minds and bodies. For forty days they prayed and fasted. At the end of their vigil they clasped hands and formed a mystic circle and listened to Rabbi Joseph pronounce God's most Sacred Name.

When he had finished the Earth trembled beneath them, thunder and lightning crashed through the Heavens above them, and the dazzling presence of the Angel Metatron appeared, surrounded by angels and seraphim. 'O sinful man!' cried Metatron, 'How dare you storm the Heavens with your prayers and oblige us to come to Earth?'

Summoning all his courage, Rabbi Joseph stood his ground.

'You must believe me when I tell you that my intentions are of the purest,' he said. 'All I want is to bring the Messiah to end the exile of the Jewish people. I beg of you to teach me how to overcome Satan's evil power.'

'Foolish man,' Metatron answered roughly, 'all your efforts are in vain. Satan is all-powerful, protected by a great wall made of the sins of the Jewish people, which God alone can penetrate. And only He will decree when the Anointed One will come. Return to your homes!'

But Rabbi Joseph remained obdurate. 'The Almighty One will give me strength to continue,' he said simply.

When Metatron saw his determination he was moved to help him. He taught the rabbi new mystic formulas and incantations with which to capture Satan and Lilith and thus banish wickedness from the world. Once that was accomplished it would leave the way free for the Messiah to come! He also showed the rabbi how to engrave God's secret Name on a metal plate. Then he spoke again. 'Listen to me. Under no circumstances must you show pity towards Satan and his wife, nor give them any food to eat or revive them with the smell of spices. If you weaken, your efforts will be wasted, and Satan will take his revenge.'

With that the angel and his host departed, and Rabbi Joseph and the five men prepared for their battle with the Evil One.

The first part of their journey led up to Mount Seir. Suddenly their way was barred by Satan's demons, who appeared in the form of a pack of vicious wild dogs, sent to frighten and confuse them. But when Rabbi Joseph pronounced an incantation they vanished.

Every step of their way was fraught with obstacles and difficulties but each time, by uttering God's holy words, they were able to overcome them.

At last, on the summit of a towering mountain, they came to a wooden hut. The moment Rabbi Joseph tried to enter, he was almost overpowered by two huge snarling hounds which sprang at his throat. Quickly he brought out the metal plate on which God's Divine Name was engraved. It acted like magic—the dogs, who were Satan and Lilith in disguise, lost their evil power and slunk away.

The five disciples bound the animals with ropes on which were tied small metal amulets engraved with the mystic Names of God. Immediately the dogs took on human appearance, except for their fiery eyes and wings.

'Please give us some food,' they whimpered, but, remembering Metatron's warning, Rabbi Joseph refused.

'Quick, we must hurry now,' Rabbi Joseph said impatiently. 'The end of our goal is in sight and soon the Gates of Heaven will open for us to welcome the Anointed One.'

All this time Satan and Lilith kept up a pitiful moan. 'Help! help! We are dying of hunger, give us something to eat.'

But Rabbi Joseph hardened his heart to their entreaties.

They tried another plea. 'Perhaps we don't deserve any food,' they whispered weakly, 'but surely you cannot refuse us just one smell of your spices. As you can see, our end is near.'

Now Rabbi Joseph was a compassionate man who could not endure suffering of any kind, in man or beast. Having triumphed over Satan and Lilith he thought the offer of a smell of the spices could do no harm.

How mistaken he was! As soon as they smelt the spices, tongues of searing flames shot from their nostrils as all their former strength returned to them. They tore away from their bonds and summoned their shrieking devils and demons to their aid.

Two of the disciples collapsed and died of fright. Two more went mad and wandered off. Only Rabbi Joseph and one disciple remained.

All the angels went into mourning and the sound of weeping was heard in the Heavens. The Messiah wept, too, and led his white horse back into its Heavenly stall. The Prophet Elijah grieved and hid the great shofar which was to have signalled the Redemption. Then the voice of the Almighty thundered:

'Listen to me, Joseph della Reyna! No human has the power to end the exile! I alone, the Eternal God, will bring about the Redemption of the Jewish people when the right time comes!'

The lost princess

There was once a king who, though he ruled wisely and well, found it hard to govern his own temper and the sound of his angry voice was often heard in the palace. The king had four sons of whom he was very proud, but his clever daughter, Princess Sari, was his heart's delight. One day the king and princess quarrelled over a trivial matter. Being alike in temperament, neither would listen to the other's point of view, and tempers flared. Then the king flew into a terrible rage and roared: 'How dare you argue with the king, get out of my sight and may the Devil take you!' Shocked by this outburst, the princess gathered up her skirts and swept out of the room.

The next morning the princess was nowhere to be found. The king was informed and an immediate and thorough search of the palace and grounds was made. It was only when he realized that the princess had disappeared without trace that he was overcome with sadness and remorse. 'Where is my beloved daughter?' he moaned. 'If only I had not lost my temper this would never had happened.'

Nathan, the king's youngest son and the closest in age to the princess, was deeply affected by the strange events. He spoke quietly to his grieving father. 'Sire, give me some money, a trusty servant, and strong horses so that I can go and find my sister. No matter how far I have to travel, and no matter how long it takes, I will bring her back to you.'

With a heavy heart the king agreed, and ordered the necessary provisions. When all the preparations had been made, the king gave his blessing, and watched sadly as Nathan set off on his quest.

Nathan and his servant travelled endlessly through the length and breadth of his own and neighbouring countries. They struggled through deep dark forests, climbed craggy mountains and crossed fast-flowing rivers. One day they reached a desert—barren and desolate as far as the eye could see. On and on they rode until the sun went down and they were forced to stop and camp for the night. While the servant was busy tending the animals, Nathan saw some lights flickering in the distance. 'Tomorrow I will ride in the direction of those lights,' he said to himself. 'It may well be a town or city or at least some form of human habitation.' When the horses were saddled early the next morning they set off towards the place where Nathan had seen the lights.

They had been riding for several hours when all at once they saw a mysterious-looking palace surrounded by guards. 'I doubt if they will let me in but I can try,' Nathan thought. With that he dismounted, left his horse in his servant's charge and walked towards the guards. To his surprise no one challenged him.

The heavy gates swung open silently and he made his way without any difficulty through many inter-connecting rooms until he reached a great hall. It was full of people laughing and chatting and in the gallery above, a group of musicians were playing. At the far end of the hall a king was seated on a jewelled throne.

Nathan felt like an invisible spectator watching a colourful pageant—no one approached him and no one spoke to him. Then the crowd fell silent as all eyes turned towards the entrance. The doors were flung open, and the queen entered and took her place on a throne next to the king. Nathan gasped in surprise for the queen was none other than his sister Sari! When she looked around her and saw Nathan his heart leaped for joy for it was clear that she had recognized him.

The music started up again, a banquet was served, and while everyone was feasting the queen came to her brother. He burst out: 'I have been searching for you so long and had almost given up hope. Why did you leave so suddenly?'

Sari sighed and answered, 'No sooner had my father uttered that terrible curse than I found myself here. This is no ordinary palace, you know, it belongs to the Evil One himself.' 'Come quickly,' said Nathan impatiently. 'I have a servant and horses waiting outside and we can soon be far away from here.'

Sari sighed. 'Alas, that is not possible. This is what you must do to rescue me. Go away from here for a whole year. During that time *think* and *hope* and *pray* to set me free. I beg of you, dear brother, do not allow your thoughts to stray. On the last day of the year you must follow these special instructions. Do not eat or drink or sleep.'

Nathan assured her that he would keep faith and return in a year's time, then left the palace.

He rode off with his servant until they reached a forest. And there for the next twelve months Nathan steadfastly carried out the princess's directions. On the last day of the year he happened to pass an apple tree which he had not noticed before. Its branches were groaning under the weight of its fine red apples. Nathan looked at them longingly and, weakened by hunger, thirst and lack of sleep, he picked a ripe apple and sunk his teeth into its crisp juicy flesh. The very next moment he slumped to the ground in a deep sleep. His servant did everything he could to wake him but Nathan slept on and on like a creature in hibernation.

Nathan's servant was still by his side when he woke from his long sleep. He was covered in shame when he realized how he had been a victim of evil temptation. 'I must put these wasted years behind me and try again to free my sister,' he vowed. And so they rode back to the devil's palace. Once again the guards allowed him to walk through the long corridors until he reached the king's chamber. Nathan was shocked to see the queen's pale sad face. 'I waited for you from dawn to dusk on the last day of the year,' she reproached him. 'Only then I realized what had happened. The powers of evil were strongest when you were at your weakest. But all is not lost if you obey my orders. Come back for me in one year and in that time *think and hope and pray to set me free*. But be warned. You can eat on the last day, but you must stay awake. On no account must you drink any wine—it will make you drowsy and it is vital that you do not sleep.' Too upset to speak, Nathan kissed her and, accompanied by his servant, returned to the forest.

And so began another year of concentrating all his prayers and hopes and thoughts on rescuing Sari and reuniting her with their father. On the very last day he saw a little spring whose waters sparkled pink in the sunlight and gave off a heady smell of wine. 'I cannot remember seeing this spring before,' Nathan told his servant, 'but I need a drink to quench my thirst.' After swallowing only one mouthful he fell into a deep sleep from which nothing could waken him, though his servant tried many times. And thus he lay sleeping for a long period of time.

One day the servant saw a carriage and horses ride into the forest. He climbed a tree and watched it stop. Princess Sari stepped out. She walked straight to the place where her brother lay sleeping and tried to wake him. 'Oh my poor dear brother,' she sobbed, 'I know how long you have suffered and struggled to set me free. The Evil One put wine in the spring water on that last day and now all is lost.' Then she wrote a hasty note, hid it in the pocket of Nathan's coat, climbed back into the carriage and drove off.

When Nathan woke at last his servant told him everything that had happened. He found Sari's letter which read: 'It was impossible to wake you. I am being taken from the palace to a golden castle on top of a crystal mountain. I implore you—come and find me.'

Nathan clutched the letter in his hand and shouted: 'I will devote the rest of my life to the search for my sister.' And with that he rewarded his faithful servant and sent him back to the king, while he set off alone to find the princess.

Nathan's travels took him to the four corners of the earth. Wherever he went he asked after a golden castle built on top of a crystal mountain but the answer was always the same—no one had ever heard of such a thing, let alone seen it. So he decided to return to the desert where he had first seen the Devil's palace. On and on he travelled and was on the point of changing direction when to his astonishment he saw a giant towering over him.

'What are you doing so far from human habitation?' boomed the giant in a friendly manner. He listened to Nathan's account of his search for the lost princess. 'In all my long years, I have not heard of such a castle. Are you sure that it really exists?' The giant asked him.

'Yes, yes, of course I am sure. It must exist *somewhere*,' Nathan insisted.

The giant thought for a moment and replied. 'I will try and help by calling on all the animals under my control. They wander over a vast distance and might have heard or seen this castle.' And as if from a hidden signal every species of animal, big and small, assembled before him. All were questioned and yet not one had seen or heard of the golden castle on the crystal mountain.

When the animals had dispersed the giant bent low and said, 'Surely you can be in no doubt now? Take my advice and go home.' But Nathan refused to consider such counsel and turned away.

The giant called after him: 'I admire your determination. Listen, go and ask my brother's help. He lives deep in the desert and commands all the birds. They may have flown over the golden castle. And take this.' And he handed Nathan a leather pouch. 'This might come in useful. There will always be sufficient gold coins in it to meet your needs.'

Nathan thanked the giant for his generous gift and continued his journey.

Punished by the stifling heat of the day and the bitter cold at night, Nathan pressed on until he found the giant's brother and explained the nature of his quest. The giant heard him out and shook his head. 'I have never heard of such a castle. Turn back while you still have strength for the return journey.'

Nathan's reply was clear. 'No. I would rather die than give up now.' The giant smiled in sympathy. 'Very well, I will ask the birds.' And suddenly the sky was black with cloud upon cloud of birds and every kind of winged creature, circling overhead and then swooping down in front of the giant. But they could not help.

'Perhaps the princess imagined a golden castle on top of a crystal mountain,' the giant remarked after the birds had flown away. 'Why don't you forget all about it and turn back,' he suggested.

'Never, never,' shouted Nathan and got up to go.

'Wait a moment,' the giant called. 'If I cannot make you change your mind, at least let me be of service to you. My brother lives a good distance from here. He rules the winds which are constantly blowing in different directions. Perhaps they may have seen the golden castle. And have this—it might assist you.' And he gave Nathan a large copper key. 'This key will unlock any door you want to open—good luck.' Nathan was delighted with this invaluable gift and pressed on to find the third giant.

The giants' help and kindness gave Nathan extra strength and courage for the long journey ahead. But he was tired and weary when he finally found the third giant. Nathan told him everything about his search for the lost princess, but like his brothers he too doubted the existence of the golden palace and it was all Nathan could do to gain his support.

'Very well,' said the giant. 'I will call the winds together and ask them, but don't blame me if you hear bad news.' So saying, the giant assembled the winds from the ends of the earth and questioned them closely about the castle. Not one of them had heard of or seen such a castle. The giant turned to Nathan.

'You must surely realize that your search ends here.'

But Nathan was defiant. 'Nothing can stop me from believing that the castle *does* exist and that the princess is waiting there for me.'

Just at that moment another wind arrived. The giant was annoyed. 'Why have you come so late and so long after the others?' he complained. 'Unfortunately I was delayed through no fault of my own,' replied the wind. 'I had to transport a king's daughter to a golden castle on top of a crystal mountain.'

There were tears of joy in Nathan's eyes when he heard this. The giant, too, was affected and murmured: 'Forgive me for having doubted you. I realize how much you must have suffered in your long search.' And he took a silver whistle out of his pocket. 'This is for you. Just blow on it if you are in danger and one of my winds will be yours to command.' And before Nathan had time to thank him properly, the giant ordered the wind to carry him to the crystal mountain.

Nathan found himself outside a well-fortified

order to gain access to the castle. He bought suitable clothing, a large bag, and an assortment of trinkets, jewellery and brightly coloured scarves to sell. Nathan decided to stay at an inn and learn from the landlord what he could about the layout of the castle and the daily routine of its household.

At last it was time to act. Dressed like a merchant with his bag full of merchandise, Nathan climbed up to the castle. He had no difficulty with the guards. On the contrary, as soon as they saw his goods, he was welcomed in. Nathan laid out his wares in the courtyard and very soon the ladies-in-waiting crowded round, eager to see what was on sale. While they were diverted, Nathan slipped away to the east wing. At the top of a steep staircase he found a locked door. The key the second giant had given him opened it easily and there, inside, was his sister Sari—the lost princess.
'You came, you came at last,' she wept.

Nathan knew that there was not a moment to lose. 'Hurry, we must get away while the ladies-in-waiting are occupied,' he said.
'Oh, but the Devil has made sure that I can never escape,' Sari said bitterly. 'Even if we were to leave this room—and you have made that possible—he would appear just as soon as our feet touched the first step. There is no other way out—other than the window and below is a sheer drop over the mountain.'

Nathan ran over to the window, opened it and cried, 'But there is another way out!' He found the little whistle, blew hard on it and within seconds a wind blew into the room.
'How can I help you?' it asked. And Nathan ordered the wind to take them back to their father, the king. And the gentle wind carried them both through the window of the Devil's castle, high over the mountain to the skies above. On and on they flew until the wind set them down in front of their father's palace.

And the king, old and frail, was there to meet them. He opened wide his arms and gathered his beloved daughter and son close to him. He could not speak, indeed there was no need for words. The light of joy and happiness which shone from his eyes expressed everything he felt.

walled city at the foot of the mountain. He had learned that the inhabitants were, like Sari, kept there under the Devil's spell. At first the soldiers on guard refused to let him pass, but after they had been well bribed with gold from the first giant's leather pouch the gates were opened and no questions asked. Just inside the city gates a busy market was in full swing. Nathan bought food and drink and found a quiet place to sit and watch while he took stock of the situation. Nearby he saw a man buy the entire contents of a fruit and vegetable stall, then order his servant to load it all into a cart and take it away.
'You look pleased with yourself,' Nathan told the stallholder.
'And I have every right to be,' he replied. 'They use only first-class produce up at the castle, and the king and queen, her ladies-in-waiting and members of the royal household are my best customers.'

This gave Nathan an idea. He planned to disguise himself as a travelling merchant in

A portion in Paradise

The word Paradise is an ancient Persian word meaning a walled garden and has come to mean a wonderful Messianic time in the future. This coming age of glory would be identical with the innocent age of the Garden of Eden long ago. Many Jews believed that Paradise was always present, but concealed, a hidden place to which the souls of the patriarchs, the chosen and the righteous people, were taken. In the course of time, it became a natural progression for Jews who believed in the immortality of the soul, in the reward of virtue and in the punishment of evil, to direct their thoughts to the *Olam Ha-Ba*, the World-to-Come.

But there was a wide variation in the way the Jewish people regarded the World-to-Come. It ranged from an abstract and spiritual realm to a very real place which could be described in great detail. According to one account: 'There are five chambers for various classes of the righteous. The first is built of cedar, with a ceiling of transparent crystal. This is the habitation for non-Jews who become true and devoted converts to Judaism. They are headed by Obadiah the prophet and Onkelos the proselyte who teach them the Law. The second is built of cedar, with a ceiling of fine silver. This is the habitation of the penitents, headed by Menasseh, King of Judah, who teaches them the Law. The third chamber is built of silver and gold, ornamanted with pearls. It is very spacious, fragrant with spices and sweet odours. The Patriarchs rest there as well as Moses and Aaron, David and Solomon, and representatives of every generation of Israel. Moses teaches them the Law. The fourth chamber is made of olive wood and is inhabited by those who have suffered for the sake of their religion. The fifth chamber is built of precious stones, gold and silver. This chamber is inhabited by the Messiah and the Prophet Elijah. Every Monday and Thursday, on Sabbaths and on holy days, the Patriarchs, Moses and Aaron and others, call on the Messiah and condole with him in the hope of the fast approaching end.'

At the other extreme, and in order to counter materialistic attitudes, Rabbi Rab, a famous rabbi, wrote in the Talmud:
'In Paradise there is no eating, no drinking, no business, no hatred or ambition; but the righteous sit with crowned heads and enjoy the radiance of the Shekina—the Divine Presence.'

The good neighbours

Everybody agreed that Rabbi Simeon was a good man. He was a sage, attended synagogue services regularly, and was steeped in the wisdom of the Torah. If he had any critics, and thankfully they were few, they might have thought him a little proud.

One day Rabbi Simeon prayed to God and asked: 'Almighty God, is there a place in the World to Come for your devout and humble servant?'

And God answered his prayer saying: 'Simeon, my son, you are a God-fearing man and you have earned the right to enter Paradise. You will be seated next to Yossele the butcher.'

Now on the one hand Rabbi Simeon was genuinely grateful to have been granted a seat in the World-to-Come, but on the other he was quite put out at the prospect of sitting next to a mere butcher.

'Yossele the butcher, indeed,' he said to himself. 'My neighbour in Paradise is to be Yossele the butcher?' he repeated in a tone of disbelief. And then he went on: 'God knows that I am a pious man. I cannot believe that having devoted my entire life to the study of the Talmud and the Torah, and reached an eminent position in this world, I will have to sit side by side with a common butcher in the next.'

The truth of the matter was that Rabbi Simeon felt utterly humiliated and his pride was well and truly hurt. No matter how hard he tried to forget about it, Yossele the butcher haunted him at every turn and preyed on the Rabbi's mind when he should have been concentrating on his religious studies.

Then gradually the rabbi's indignation changed to curiosity. 'I wonder what kind of man this butcher is,' he thought. 'It would be better for my own peace of mind to find out if he deserves to be by my side in Heaven.'

The decision was made and it was with a sense of relief tinged with apprehension that Rabbi Simeon called on Yossele the butcher. The butcher was rich and hospitable and was genuinely delighted when the rabbi agreed to be his guest for a few days. During his stay Yossele

conferred every honour due to his learned guest and nothing was too much trouble to ensure that the rabbi was happy and comfortable.

One day Rabbi Simeon invited the butcher to accompany him on a long walk. After a while he asked him: 'Tell me, Yossele, are you a pious man?'

Yossele replied: 'I am sorry to say that I have badly neglected my religious duties. Instead of devoting time to the study of the Torah I have invested all my energies in business affairs. I have worked long hours and my profits and prospects are very good.' Then he smiled at the rabbi. 'I may not be perfect, but neither am I altogether a bad man,' he said, and continued, 'I have never turned away anyone in need and every Friday I provide the poor people of this and neighbouring towns with meat for the Sabbath day.'

Rabbi Simeon listened respectfully but remained unimpressed. He regarded the giving of charity as an integral part of Jewish life, and not something which would give a distinguished rabbi and an ordinary butcher equal status in the World-to-Come. No, he was definitely not satisfied and questioned the butcher further.

'Well,' said the rabbi, 'I am sure that the poor benefit from your generosity. But have you done anything else that is praiseworthy?' he asked.

Yossele was silent for a while. 'No, not really,' he said honestly, 'I cannot recall anything that would be considered particularly commendable.'

Then as an afterthought he said, 'But you might like to hear how I was once caught up in a series of unusual circumstances. It happened during the time when I was a customs officer for this city. Whenever a ship anchored in the harbour, it was my job to go on board, examine the cargo and collect the customs duty.

'One day I boarded a ship which had just anchored offshore and the captain told me he had a special cargo for sale and asked me if I would like to buy it.

'I told him I would have to see what he was selling before I decided and, to my horror he brought up.on deck a hundred Jewish slaves in chains.

'"How much do you want for them?" I asked the captain, disguising my feelings of pity and compassion for my poor downtrodden brothers and sisters.

'"The price is a real bargain for a quick sale because I need the space in the hold for fresh supplies. But if you are not interested, I will have to throw them overboard and get rid of them quickly that way," he said.

'Although I was not as wealthy as I am now, I managed to find the money to buy them all. Then I paid the captain, brought the slaves ashore, fed and clothed them and even managed to find them lodgings. In time I paired off the young people, provided dowries for the girls, and witnessed their weddings according to Jewish law.

'However, there was one very beautiful girl among the slaves who stood out from the rest. She had a quiet dignity in spite of all the dangers and difficulties she had experienced. I was so taken with her that I arranged a match between her and my son.

'A wedding feast was prepared and I invited all the townsfolk, including all the former Jewish slaves. There was great rejoicing and feasting and everyone seemed to be enjoying themselves. But there was one exception. I noticed one of the freed slaves sitting by himself with his head down and his hands covering his face.

'"Why are you sitting here on your own?" I asked him. But he did not reply. I tried again: "Come along and join in the festivities. This is a wedding party, you know." But instead of an answer I heard an anguished sob, and the young man wept as if his heart would break.

'I sat down beside him and waited until he was able to speak. "On the very day that we were rounded up and sold into slavery," said the young man brushing away his tears, "I was to have married the beautiful girl who is now married to your son."

'I felt deeply for the poor young man, but there was nothing I could do to help him. "You must forget all about her now and marry one of the nice single girls in the community. As soon as you have made your choice I will pay for all the wedding expenses."

'He turned on me angrily. "Gold and silver have no meaning for me. If I was given all the money in the world I could not stop loving the girl I was to marry. And now she is your son's wife." And the tears welled up in his eyes again and rolled down his cheeks.

'The young man was inconsolable and his grief touched me so much that I went to my son and explained everything to him. When I had finished I could see that he, too, was deeply moved.

'"Father I am glad you have told me this," he said. "I would always feel a sense of guilt if I was responsible for keeping the young couple apart. I will divorce my wife so that she can be free to wed the man she loves."

'And that is exactly what happened. The two lovers were married and I gave the young girl a handsome dowry.'

There was just a hint of dampness in the rabbi's eyes when the butcher had finished recounting his story.

That night he prayed to God: 'Praise be to the Almighty God. Forgive me for having doubted Your Wisdom. It will be a special blessing and a great honour to have a place in Paradise—next to Yossele the butcher.'

Bontshe the Silent

Bontshe's death made no lasting impression whatsoever. The whole affair was conducted as silently as the grave itself. There were no coffin bearers, no mourners at the funeral, no one to grieve or to wipe away tears of sorrow. With no kith or kin, Bontshe the Silent died alone.

After the funeral, the wind swept away the small wooden board which marked his grave. The grave-digger's wife found it some distance away and used it to make a fire to boil her pot of potatoes. And three days later the grave-digger was hard put to remember the unmarked spot where Bontshe was buried.

It would be pointless to ask, 'Who was Bontshe? How did he live? Or what did he die of?' Was it heart failure? An incurable disease? A broken heart? The heavy burden of hunger and poverty?—the list is long but the answer is brief—no one knows.

Bontshe had lived quietly and died without a murmur. He passed like a shadow over the face of the earth. His birth was uneventful, his circumcision equally so—no celebrations, no wine, no clinking of glasses to toast *le chaim*— to life. As for his thirteenth birthday—his bar-mitzvah—to honour his entry into the adult Jewish world—that left no impact on anyone, least of all himself. He lived like some dull grain of sand on the seashore, merging without trace among the millions of its kind.

He left no personal effects, no property, no children—nothing. He had lived miserably and he died in like manner. Had the world not been too busy with more important matters, someone might have noticed that even during his lifetime Bontshe's eyes were sunken, and his cheeks painfully hollow. Whether or not he was carrying a load on his back, he walked with a permanent stoop, his head bent to the ground as if looking for his own grave.

When he was taken to hospital, Bontshe's 'home'—a corner of a cold, damp basement—was immediately occupied by someone else. Ten poor people like Bontshe had haggled over it and it had been sold to the highest bidder. And when Bontshe's body was carried to the mortuary, there were twenty poor patients waiting for his empty hospital bed. A quiet birth, a quiet life, a quiet death, and an even quieter burial.

But as for his reception in the Other World, that was altogether a different matter! Over there the announcement of Bontshe's death created little short of a sensation. The mighty trumpet sound of the Messianic shofar—the ram's horn—vibrated and echoed throughout the seven heavens. Archangels flew about announcing the news with great excitement: 'Bontshe the Silent has died! He has been summoned to appear before the Supreme Court of Judgement! Bontshe is to take his place in the Heavenly Academy.'

The ripples of sheer pleasure and excitement flowed through Paradise and a great shout went up: 'Bontshe the Silent is coming—Bontshe is on his way!'

A band of young angels with eyes that sparkled like diamonds, rushed about in readiness to meet him. The buzzing of their gossamer wings, the patter of their silver-slippered feet, the music of their merry laughter filled the heavens until it reached the throne of the Most High.

The Patriarch Abraham stood ready at the heavenly gates, with arms outstretched in welcome. 'Shalom Aleichem, peace be with you, Bontshe,' and his sweet smile lit up the finely drawn features of his wrinkled face.

And the happy throng parted to allow two angels to bring in a chair made of pure gold —ready for Bontshe's comfort, and a gold crown, set with sparkling precious stones— to place on his head.

The saints were surprised at all the activity and excitement and not a little envious. 'Why all these preparations before the decision of the Heavenly Court has been given?' they asked pointedly.
'And why ever not?' the angels retorted, 'after all the judgement will be a mere formality. The Prosecutor cannot possibly have a word to say against Bontshe. It will be an open and shut case—no more than five minutes at the outset. After all Bontshe the Silent is held in the highest regard here.'

As for Bontshe—siezed in mid-air by little angels, greeted personally by the Patriarch Abraham, seated gently on his chair, and the gold crown placed on his head—it was all much too much for him. He was sure it was all some dreadful mistake or a dream from which he would soon be roughly awakened. He sat nervously perched on the edge of his seat, afraid to move or to speak, eyes on the ground too frightened to look up.

And then he started to tremble. 'Supposing,' he thought, 'they are expecting a wealthy man, an eminent rabbi or even a saint? As soon as he arrives, I will be blamed for this terrible mistake and. . .' And all kinds of cruel punishments flashed across his mind. He became so engrossed he was unaware of the angels' compliments, hardly noticed their beautiful dancing, and did not respond to Abraham's cordial greeting. By the time he was brought in to the celestial court he was simply beside himself with fear.

Nor did he hear the President of the Court call out: 'The case of Bontshe the Silent!'

Then above the muffled voices in the great hall Bontshe began to distinguish more clearly the soft angelic voice of the advocate.
'This man has never uttered a word of complaint against God or man. There was never a spark of hatred in his eyes, nor did he make claims on heaven.'
'What is he talking about?' Bontshe muttered to himself, completely mystified. Then he heard the President's harsh voice interrupt the speaker. 'We can do without the flowery descriptions, thank you.'

The advocate continued, 'In my view, Bontshe the Silent has suffered even more than Job in the Bible.'
'Facts, please keep to the facts,' called the President.
'He kept silent,' the advocate continued, 'when, at the tender age of thirteen, his mother died and a cruel stepmother took her place.'
'Perhaps they mean me,' thought Bontshe to himself.
'She begrudged him every mouthful, even stale, mouldy bread, while she drank coffee with cream.'

'Kindly keep to the subject,' the President ordered.
'But she never spared him her fingernails, or cuffs and body blows, and his black and blue body which showed through the holes of his threadbare clothes was proof of her cruelty. In winter he had to stand barefoot in the biting frost to chop wood although he was barely strong enough to wield the heavy axe. Bontshe remained silent before her and his father.'
'Oh yes, that drunkard,' laughed the accusing lawyer, and Bontshe felt cold all over.
'Bontshe was always alone. He had no friends, no schooling, no religious instruction, no decent clothes and never a free moment.'

The President began to get irritated. 'I do wish you would keep to the facts,' he complained.
'And later he kept silent when his father, drunk and abusive, grabbed him by the hair and threw him out of the house on a freezing cold winter's night. Without a word he picked himself up out of the snow and ran as far away fom his home as he could get.
'On and on he went, stopping only when the gnawing pangs of hunger made him too weak to continue. Then he begged—not with words—but by the eloquent message in his sad eyes.
'Friendless, starving, he reached the big town where he was desperate to find work in order to survive. He finally found a back-breaking job for which he was paid a pittance. Even when he was crushed under the weight of the great loads he had to carry, Bontshe kept silent. He was splashed with mud, spat on, driven with his heavy pack from the pavements into the street among the cabs, carts and coaches, staring death in the face at every turn. He never calculated how little he was paid, how many errands he had to run, and how many times he was almost killed on his way to collect his wages.

And he never insisted loudly on his pay— he just stood in the doorway like a beggar. He was often told to come back later. He would disappear like a shadow and when he returned he would ask for his wages even more humbly than before. He made no murmur when they cheated him or threw in a counterfeit coin. He remained silent!'

'They really do mean me after all,' Bontshe thought.

The advocate paused for a sip of water, then continued. 'Then Bontshe's life changed. One day he saw a carriage careering down the road out of control. It was drawn by two terrified runaway horses, galloping along at breakneck speed, sparks flying from their hoofs and foam streaming from their mouths. Somehow he managed to stop them and cling on to them and calm them down. The driver, who had been thrown off the coach, lay with a cracked skull some distance away, and the owner, a wealthy Jew, was inside, suffering from shock.

Fortunately the Jew was a charitable man, duly grateful to Bontshe for saving his life. He not only made him his coachman, but provided him with a wife.'

'There is no doubt about it, they are talking about me,' Bontshe assured himself, but he still lacked the courage to look up at the Heavenly Court. Nevertheless although his eyes remained lowered, he went on listening intently to the soft sad voice of his defending angel.

'Bontshe did not protest when his protector became bankrupt and stopped his wages, and his wife deserted him. He said nothing when he heard later that his former benefactor had paid off all his creditors except himself.

'One day he was knocked down and run over by the self-same carriage he used to drive. He had good cause to scream in agony and pain but his lips were tightly sealed.

'He was taken to hospital but he did not complain when the doctor refused to examine him without first being paid fifteen kopeks, nor when the attendant refused to change his bed linen until he was given five.

'He was silent in his death agony, and he was silent in his last hour. He never once uttered a word against God, or his fellow man. And that concludes my defence.'

Once again Bontshe was seized with a fit of trembling when he realized it was now the turn of the prosecution. 'What will they say about me?' he wondered. He did not remember much about his own life—it had been described in every detail by the angel advocate. 'But what will the prosecuting angel have to say?'

'Gentlemen judges,' the Prosecutor began in a strident voice and then stopped. Bontshe gripped the sides of his chair.

'Gentlemen,' he began again, and this time he spoke softly. 'Gentlemen judges! Bontshe was silent! I shall be silent too!'

A gentle hush descended on the entire court. Then a new sweet melodious voice was heard from above: 'Bontshe, my child, Bontshe my dearest child.'

And just when he really wanted to look up, his eyes were brimming with tears—tears of joy. Never in his life had he experienced such sweet emotion before. And not since his mother had died had anyone spoken to him so kindly.

'My child,' continued the presiding judge, 'you have suffered and kept silent, there is not one part of your body that has escaped a wound or a scar, and not a fibre of your soul that has not bled; and you have always kept silent.

'Down below on earth no one understood these things because you lived in a world of falsehood, whilst here in Heaven in the world of truth, you will reap your reward.' Then there was a pause while everyone waited for the final verdict.

'Bontshe, the Heavenly Court will not judge you, nor will it pass sentence on you. You may have anything your heart desires.'

For the first time Bontshe looked up. The splendour of his surroundings and the brilliant lights dazzled him so much that he dropped his weary gaze once more. 'Really?' he asked shyly.

'Yes, really,' replied the President of the Celestial Tribunal. 'Everything in Heaven belongs to you because all that shines and sparkles is only the reflection of your hidden goodness.'

'Really?' Bontshe asked again, with a new confidence in his voice.

'But of course, most certainly,' everyone assured him.

'Well, in that case,' Bontshe said with a happy smile, 'I should like to have a hot freshly baked roll and butter every day for breakfast.'

The court and the angels looked down, a little embarrassed. The Prosecutor burst out laughing.

Symbols in the stories

At the beginning of each chapter Edward Ripley has illustrated some of the symbols and characters appearing in the stories. The following notes describe the items in each illustration, starting at the top.

p.7 THE JEWISH HERITAGE The seven-branched candlestick or Menorah. A seven-branched lamp was used in the Temple at Jerusalem and is still used in the synagogue. The seven lights symbolize the days of the week or the seven spheres. The scrolls represent the Torah, the written law. The six-pointed Star of David or 'the Shield of David' has been known since the seventh century BCE. It became a specific Jewish symbol in the 19th century. Below these are the three rows of four semi-precious stones worn as part of the priest's clothing specified in the Book of Leviticus. The man is wearing a phylactery (a small box containing pieces of parchment on which verses from the Bible are written) and a prayer shawl. These are worn by observant Jews at both formal and informal prayers. At the bottom is the facade of the Temple in Jerusalem, from a wall painting dated about 250 CE.

p.11 THE CREATION The world, with the sun, moon and stars. Below are the letters of the Hebrew alphabet, which begins with the letter Aleph and reads from right to left. Below these are the wave which was held back by the grains of sand, the tree of knowledge and Adam and Eve with birds, animals and insects in the Garden of Eden.

p.16 THE GREAT FLOOD Noah's ark before its launch, and some of the animals rescued from the Flood. Below is the rainbow that symbolized God's promise not to destroy mankind again and the dove returning to the Ark with an olive branch. The Ark aground on Mount Ararat, with the raven, the first bird that was sent out to report whether the Flood was receding.

p.21 THE PATRIARCHS Pagan idols smashed by Abraham. The idol here is based on a Canaanite clay statue and is thought to represent a mother goddess from Iron Age Palestine (12th century BCE). Below: a nomadic tent with sheep and goats. The design of these tents has probably changed little since Bible times. The bowl of lentil stew for which Esau exchanged his birthright. Bottom: Joseph's dreams—the dreams that enraged his brothers with, above these, the two dreams he interpreted in Pharaoh's prison.

p.32 MOSES, THE GREAT LEADER The infant Moses in a papyrus cradle, based on the design of ancient Egyptian papyrus boats. The stylized papyrus frond is typical of Egyptian decoration. Below is the burning bush and loaves of flat bread, baked without yeast, the originals of the matzos eaten at the festival of Passover. The parting of the Red Sea. Quails, which were

141

food for the Israelites in the wilderness. The Golden Calf, based on a statuette from the period, when bull worship was common. Bottom: Moses' miraculous staff.

p.41 HEROES AND HEROINES Samson pulls down the pillars of the Philistine's temple. Below, the bees whose honey Samson collected from the nest in a lion's skull. Ruth gleaning, picking up the stalks left behind by the harvesters. The two elders who plotted Susanna's disgrace.

p.49 THE KINGS David as a boy with his harp and, below, the sling and stones with which he defeated Goliath. Below are items from the stories about King Solomon: the old woman's miraculous bag of flour; the bee that stung King Solomon's nose, with the other insects he summoned; the tree house in which Penina was imprisoned; the hoopoe with the shamir. The jar at the bottom is based on a storage jar from the 8th or 9th centuries BCE, the time of the early Israelite kings. The widow in 'The silent witnesses' could have hidden her money in a jar like this.

p.62 THE PROPHETS Elijah fed by ravens and, below, carried to heaven in a fiery chariot. Below this is the treasure that lay hidden beneath the gatepost in the story 'The Prophet's pupil' and the cup of Elijah—the cup of wine provided for Elijah, the herald of the Messiah, at Passover time. The figure below is Elijah, disguised as a poor traveller, the form in which he was said to move about the world unrecognized. Bottom: Jonah with the whale and the gourd tree, the vehicles of God's messages to him.

p.70 TALES FROM THE TALMUD The scrolls of the Talmud with, below, a rabbi or teacher explaining their meanings. Below: The circle Honi drew in the sand as he prayed for rain, with the cloud that brought rain, and the fruit of the carob tree which grew up while he slept. Below this is the water trickling over the rock from which Akiba learned the lesson of perseverance and the willows where the Israelites hung their harps before going into exile in Babylon. At the bottom is the harvest equally divided between the two loving brothers and the Temple that was built on the site of their field.

p.86 LEGENDS FROM THE MIDDLE AGES The head of the pious ox, who refused to work on the Sabbath; the Sultan's ring from the story 'Asking the impossible'; Leviathan and the clever fox; the miser's empty plate and the key to his box of treasure. Bottom: the Golem, with the fish and the applecart he carried home.

p.105 RABBIS AND MIRACLES Top and right: The demon's stretching arm. Below this is a Hasidic rabbi with characteristic beaver hat. Book-binding tools and angels look down on the book-binder's Sabbath table ('Rabbi Israel laughs three times') with the chollahs (Sabbath loaves of plaited bread topped with poppyseed), wine and candles. The loaves symbolize the manna with which the Children of Israel were fed in the wilderness. On the table, they are covered with a cloth to symbolize the protective covering of dew which settled on them; the 2 candles symbolize the two biblical commands 'remember' and 'observe'. Wine symbolizes blessing and joy. Bottom: The magic flowers that enabled the Ba'al Shem Tov to cure the princess ('King David's scroll'), and the cave in which he found them.

p.113 TALES OF THE FESTIVALS Triangular hamantaschen, small cakes traditionally baked at Purim, the festival of Queen Esther. Harvest festival offerings, standing for the festival of Sukkoth. Queen Esther with, below, greggers or rattles, used to drown out the name of Haman when the scrolls of Esther are read at Purim. Bottom: an ancient Hanukkah lamp, with its 8 lights, symbolizing the 8 days which a single day's supply of oil lasted, keeping the rededicated lamp of the Temple alight.

p.122 TALES OF LONGING The apples which tempted the prince to eat and so fail to rescue his sister ('The lost princess'). Below this, the angel Sandalfon who appeared to Joseph della Reyner, with Satan and Lilith, transformed into raving dogs. The crystal mountain on which the lost princess was found and the animals the first giant called upon to ask how to find it. Bottom: the Messiah's white horse, ready to carry the Messiah to earth if Joseph della Reyner should succeed in his efforts.

p.134 A PORTION IN PARADISE Paradise imagined as a walled Middle Eastern garden with, below, Elijah sounding the shofar, the ram's horn trumpet which will announce the coming of the Messiah. The shofar is sounded on New Year and at the end of Yom Kippur, the Day of Atonement. Below this are angels, the gates of paradise, and Bontshe's fresh roll and butter.

Index